ALASTAIR SAWDAY'S
SPECIAL PLACES TO STAY

BRITISH
HOLIDAY
HOMES

At last – our independent guide to self-catering
  properties in Britain, selected with taste, panache
and bravura. Trust us, and enjoy them.

Design: Caroline King

Maps & Mapping: Bartholomew Mapping, a division of HarperCollins,
                Glasgow

Printing: Canale, Italy

UK Distribution: Portfolio, Greenford, Middlesex

US Distribution: The Globe Pequot Press, Guilford, Connecticut

Published in November 2002

Alastair Sawday Publishing Co. Ltd
The Home Farm Stables, Barrow Gurney, Bristol BS48 3RW
Tel: +44 (0)1275 464891 Fax: +44 (0)1275 464887
E-mail: info@specialplacestostay.com Web: www.specialplacestostay.com

The Globe Pequot Press
P. O. Box 480, Guilford, Connecticut 06437, USA
Tel: +1 203 458 4500 Fax: +1 203 458 4601
E-mail: info@globe-pequot.com Web: www.globe-pequot.com

First edition

Copyright © November 2002 Alastair Sawday Publishing Co. Ltd

A catalogue record for this book is available from the British Library.

Alastair Sawday has asserted his right to be identified as the author of this work.

ISBN 1-901970-30-2 in the UK
ISBN 0-7627-2459-5 in the US

Printed in Italy

The publishers have made every effort to ensure the accuracy of the information
in this book at the time of going to press. However, they cannot accept any
responsibility for any loss, injury or inconvenience resulting from the use of
information contained therein.

ALASTAIR SAWDAY'S
SPECIAL PLACES TO STAY

BRITISH
HOLIDAY
HOMES

The
Globe
Pequot
Press

Guilford
Connecticut, USA

ALASTAIR
SAWDAY
PUBLISHING

Alastair Sawday Publishing
Bristol, UK

CONTENTS

Acknowledgements • A word from Alastair Sawday

Introduction • General map • Maps

england

CONTENTS

wales

scotland

See the back of the book for:

- Farmers' Markets • Cycle hire shops • Pubs & Inns
- What is Alastair Sawday Publishing?
- www.specialplacestostay.com
- Alastair Sawday Special Places to Stay series • Little Earth Book
- Report form • Quick reference indices • Index by place name
- Exchange rates • Explanation of symbols

ACKNOWLEDGEMENTS

Horse-designing committees don't always, it seems, come up with camels. Half of this publishing company has worked on this book and the result is triumphantly similar to our original design. Johnathan Goodall began, with his usual dependable decency, and was followed by Nicola Crosse who took over the reins until a hospital operation; she battled heroically right up to the last barricade. Kerry Burns, once her main support system, then became the pillar of that particular establishment. Laura Kinch was the quiet, but active, string-puller providing continuity throughout the performance. The writing was put in the hands of the ever-competent Jo Boissevain who has pulled rabbits out of hats – it is less easy to write vividly when human beings play lesser roles, unlike in B&Bs where they are so fundamental to the character of the places.

Kim Lawrence and Lucinda Carling were stoic and inspired inspectors. Jackie King – whose energy should have been sapped by her work on British B&B – gently, and with massive competence, helped steer the whole project to completion. Julia Richardson and her able production team (below) provided the last piece of the jigsaw.

So, a grand team effort and I doff my cycling helmet to them all.

Alastair Sawday

Series Editor:	Alastair Sawday
Editorial Team:	Jo Boissevain, Kerry Burns, Nicola Crosse, Laura Kinch, Jackie King
Editorial Director:	Annie Shillito
Production Manager:	Julia Richardson
Web Producer:	Russell Wilkinson
Production Assistants:	Rachel Coe, Tom Dalton, Paul Groom
Accounts:	Bridget Bishop
Photo of Alastair Sawday:	Fiona Duby
Country photos:	Michael Busselle
Inspections:	Jan Adams, Lucinda Carling, Sally Collier, Trish Dugmore, Jonathon Goodall, Kim Lawrence, Hazel Leutchford, Tom Pinsent, Bruce Smith.
Additional writing:	Jonathan Goodall, Christopher Somerville, Anne Woodford

A special thank you, too, to other inspectors who saw just one or two houses for us – often at short notice.

A WORD FROM
ALASTAIR SAWDAY

Baked beans on toast,
catering sausages,
porridge, eggs
from battery hens and
feckless, pasty-faced
youths ladling it all
out – that's the
scene that the word
'catering' evokes in this
particular mind.
So we were reluctant
to use 'Self-catering'
for the title of this book!
Brains were wracked
for alternatives
and 'holiday homes'
was the result.

I had a hellish self-catering holiday once, a pokey flat in Wales which I had assumed to be bigger, prettier and with views. Every inch of it was grim, from the electric fire to the nylon sheets. The place was mean-spirited, designed to screw every last penny out of us, for as little effort as possible. Our hearts sank lower and lower – and we left. I determined to produce a book about decent places – one day.

Our French Holiday Homes guide has now blazed a trail and given readers a choice of gorgeous places to spend their precious holidays. Let us do the same for you in the UK, where there are thousands and thousands of holiday homes to choose from – but how on earth do you know whom to trust when reading brochures and web sites?

Take the case of Amanda Craig, the journalist who was lured with her family to a seductively described holiday house in the Lot, in France. She wrote 'My holiday hell in the land of plastic chairs' in *The Sunday Times* in August this year. The family abandoned the expensive, plastic-furnished house after two days and wandered disconsolately back to Britain, saved – as it happens – from total despair only by our Hotels guide. If only, as she admits, she had known about our book.

So, your week in your own holiday home is precious; you cannot afford to get it wrong. With more and more of us choosing to stay in Britain for our holidays rather than risk delays and chaos on the way overseas, this is a good time to begin helping you to find the right place. We have developed, much to our delight, a reputation for being totally trustworthy. And, just as importantly, we are known for our 'taste'. It may not, to the relief of our readers, always be 'good' taste in the conventional sense, but it will always be interesting, often magnificent. And we do tell the truth about every place we have selected, for they are not all perfect in every way. So here it is, our first stab at showing you some of Britain's most attractive places to rent for your holidays.

Alastair Sawday

INTRODUCTION

You hold in your hand a rare thing: a guidebook containing a hand-picked selection of self-catering properties, all (save just one or two, and these are marked) visited by us, chosen for you. We want this guide to be your shining light in a market that's crammed with misleading advertising and limited, independent advice. It follows on from our guide to French Holiday Homes that has proved so successful.

We've all, when pondering our holidays, ploughed through chunky agency brochures, undiscerning web sites and tourist board information in an effort to find the perfect holiday house, but are often hindered by lack of independent opinion. Each and every place, the brochures would have us believe, is idyllic. Getting it right has, until now, been more a matter of luck than judgement.

Well, uncross your fingers; you now have us to guide you. There are 115 honest descriptions of properties here. Many of them belong to owners who feature in our Bed & Breakfast book, so know them well and feel sure that they, and each of the other owners, will go to great lengths to make sure you enjoy your stay.

Many owners live on site – sometimes in the house next door – and some live elsewhere yet will have things in place to give you a good welcome and a warm house.

There should be something for everyone – whether you're part of a couple that wants to be in glorious isolation or parents of young children who prefer to be in a sociable setting with other families. We have windmills with watery scenery, an old mine count-house perched above the Tamar, a Jacobean banqueting hall on top of a hill, a loft-style apartment in… Halifax. And there's also a cottage with a terraced garden that gives onto a view said by Ruskin to be "one of the loveliest in England". There are also townhouses, slick city boltholes, rustic barns and impossibly pretty cottages, dotted throughout England, Scotland and Wales.

If a handful are, perhaps, slightly functional they are included because they are in a peaceful, stunning setting with glorious walks that start from the door. Many have been chosen because they are stylishly comfortable and characterful and your every need has been anticipated.

INTRODUCTION

Finding the right place for you

Do read our write-ups carefully – we want to guide you to a place where you'll feel happy. If you are staying on a farm, don't be surprised to have tractors passing at seven in the morning, or to hear the farmer calling his cattle for milking.

An ancient building may have temperamental plumbing and be less than hermetically sealed against draughts; a remote hilltop cottage may have power cuts. Would you worry about lighting candles with your toddler crashing about?

Use our descriptions as a taster of what is on offer – we only have around 200 words to tell a whole story – and have a conversation with the owner about the finer details. Perhaps we've mentioned a pool and you might want to check that it will be heated at Easter or to ask whether the bikes will be available on your particular weekend.

If the entry says in italics at the end, "6 other cottages available, too", do realise that you may not be in glorious isolation, but will perhaps be cheek-by-jowl with other guests and their families, cars, children, comings and goings, etc. This shouldn't spoil your holiday but, if absolute peace is vital, ask the owner how many other people are likely to be around.

Consider, too, that you may be out of reach for a few days; many of these places will not have reception for any mobile phone network. If staying in touch with the outside world is a necessity, again check with the owner.

How to use this book

Finding the houses

If you are looking for a house in a particular bit of Britain, use our maps at the front of the book, see what we have in the area, then look up each property by using the entry number given on the map flags. Don't search by using the county headings at the top of each page – you may think you only want a house in Devon, but the perfect place may be less than a mile away over the border in Dorset. Searching only by county is limiting.

Our maps

The General Map is marked with the page numbers of the detailed maps. The latter show roughly where each property is. Use them as a guide only and take a proper road atlas with you.

INTRODUCTION

The addresses

We list abbreviated addresses for each property. The exact position and directions along with other details about the property will be given when booking. At the bottom of each page are owners' contact details.

How many does it sleep?

Understanding this bit is vital to your comfort!

If we say 'Sleeps: 4-6', this means the place sleeps four people comfortably, yet it can sleep six. The two extra places may be on a sofabed or, say, on camp beds on a mezzanine level. If you squeeze in the maximum number don't be surprised if space feels limited.

We do mention bunk beds – many owners put them there for children; but if you want to sleep adults in them, check with the owner first. It's important to confirm in advance how many people will be staying. Squeeze in more than you've said you will and you could be painfully squashed or, worse, in breach of contract.

Bedrooms

In this book a double means one double bed; a twin, two single beds (you may be able to link them). A triple is any mix of beds and needs to be discussed with the owner. Extra beds and cots for children can often be provided, sometimes at extra cost, so do ask.

Bathrooms

If we mention a bedroom and a bathroom without punctuation in between this means the room is en suite, eg:

1 double with shower; 1 twin with bath.

If there is punctuation in between the list of rooms, they are not en suite, eg:

1 double; 1 twin; shower; wc. (This also means the shower and wc are separate; 'shower and wc' would mean they are in the same room.)

Facilities

If it is important to you that your holiday home has a dishwasher/TV/CD-player/barbecue, check with the owners first. Most properties will have a washing machine; others may have shared laundry facilities.

INTRODUCTION

Prices

All prices are per property per week. We give a range from the cheapest, low-season, price to the highest, high-season price. Many owners offer weekend rates out of season and these places carry a Weekend Break symbol. Check with the owner and confirm in writing the price for the number of your party. These are prices for 2003 and some will increase significantly for 2004. This book is set to last for two years; check our web site for updates.

Winter lets

Most places are open all year round and are considerably cheaper in winter (except, perhaps, for Christmas and New Year). Do consider low-season holidays – you get all the comfort and scenery and no crowds or traffic jams.

Bed and Breakfast

If the owner also runs a bed and breakfast on site, we've given them the B&B symbol. Some of these owners offer evening meals at the main house or, when arranged in advance, will bring cooked suppers to you. These places are good options if you're travelling with a mixed-age group: some folk like to install granny and grandad in the B&B and keep the self-catering quarters as a family base.

There will be times when you will welcome the proximity of owners and times when you may wish for more privacy and isolation; bear this in mind when choosing.

Symbols

Symbols and their explanations are listed on the last page of the book. They are based on information given to us by the owners. Things do change, however: the bikes may no longer be roadworthy; the pool may be undergoing repair; the local grocer may have closed; the linen service may no longer be offered. Do check these things on the phone when booking. Use our symbols as a guide, not as a statement of fact.

Practical Matters

When to go

Go in the school holidays and you may feel the whole world has gone with you; however, you will have longer days, more sunshine, etc. Book a cottage in the winter and although you'll enjoy quicker journey times and fewer people you may also find far fewer restaurants to dine in or shops to browse.

INTRODUCTION

How to book

Read our descriptions, find the place best for you, check out their web site (if they have one and if you can), then contact the person listed under 'Booking details' and they will be able to answer all your questions.

Deposit and payment

Most owners will ask for a 25% deposit immediately – this is usually non-refundable – and settlement of the full bill around eight weeks before you arrive. Until you have paid the full amount your booking will not be confirmed. If you are booking less than eight weeks in advance you will normally be asked to pay the full amount immediately. A travel insurance policy may help you should you need to cancel a booking.

It is normal for owners to charge a refundable security/damage deposit payable in advance. If everything appears in order after your departure your money will be refunded; if you've spilt red wine on the cream carpet or crockery has been broken you may be charged for cleaning/replacement. Do mention any mishap to the owners – accidents happen but they would much prefer to be told about them rather than discover them later.

What payment covers

Water, gas and electricity are usually covered by the 'rent'. If they are not, the owner should tell you so in advance. Some owners have meters which are read at the beginning and end of your stay and then you are charged accordingly.

Linen is not included unless the property has the 'linen' symbol. So if there is no symbol, take your own towels, tea towels, sheets, pillowcases; if in any doubt, check when booking.

Changeover day

This is usually Saturday but varies, so do check. It is normal to arrive around 4pm and leave by 10am to give the owners/cleaners a chance to prepare the place for the next guests.

What to take

Everything you need – the essentials – should be there. But it can be the little things that make a difference to your comfort and happiness: perhaps your favourite pillow, candles to help soften the ambiance if rooms are brightly lit, your own stove-top coffee pot for your perfect breakfast, bubble bath, good

INTRODUCTION

maps of the area, board games (check if these are there), a
radio... all little things that can make a place feel more homely.

Children

Our 'Children welcome' symbol means that children of all
ages are welcome although the owner may not have all the
paraphernalia that you need for peace of mind and your child's
comfort and safety. There will often be so much for children to
explore and you must check danger spots with the owner –
a hidden pond, a river, a highly-strung dog, geese, farmyard
equipment, etc. Some owners offer to babysit or can find you
a local sitter.

Pets

Look for the 'Guests' pets welcome' symbol and check with the
owner that your furry/feathered friend is acceptable. Obviously
you are responsible for keeping your pet under control and
clearing up after it; what you find endearing/playful behaviour
could upset other guests or landowners or their animals.

Business days and hours

If heading for an out-of-the-way place, do plan your shopping in
advance. Many shops will close for lunch and have shorter
opening hours than in towns, shorter still out of holiday
seasons. It may be possible to have deliveries of some items –
bread, milk, fuel etc, so ask the owner.

Farmers' markets

You'll find a mention of these at the back of the book – they
are food markets where the farmer brings and sells his own
produce. Check out the National Association of Farmers'
Markets websites for more details: www.nafm.net

Subscriptions   Owners pay to appear in this guide; their fee goes towards
the huge costs of a sophisticated inspection system and the
production of an all-colour book. We only include places and
owners that we find positively special. It is absolutely not
possible for owners to buy their way in!

Internet   Our web site www.specialplacestostay.com has online entries
for all the places featured here and in our other books, with
up-to-date information and direct links to their own e-mail
addresses and web sites. You'll find more about the site at the
back of this book.

INTRODUCTION

Environment   We try to reduce our impact on the environment by:

- planting trees. We are officially Carbon Neutral®. The emissions directly related to paper production, printing and distribution of this book have been 'neutralised' through the planting of indigenous woodlands with Future Forests.
- re-using paper, recycling stationery, tins, bottles, etc.
- encouraging staff use of bicycles (they're loaned free) and encouraging car sharing.
- celebrating the use of organic, home – and locally-produced food.
- publishing books that support, in however small a way, the rural economy and small-scale businesses.
- running an Environmental Benefit Trust to stimulate business interest in the environment.
- We publish The Little Earth Book (www.littleearth.co.uk), a collection of essays on environmental issues. We also have a new title in production called The Little Food Book, another hard-hitting analysis – this time of the food industry.

Disclaimer   We make no claims to pure objectivity in judging our Special Places to Stay. They are here because we like them. Our opinions and tastes are ours alone and this book is a statement of them; we hope you will share them. We have done our utmost to get our facts right but apologise for any mistakes that may have crept in. Sometimes, prices shift, usually upwards.

Do let us know how you get on in these places – reader feedback is crucial and helps keep us up to date with changes. Poor reports are immediately followed up with the owner (no mention is made of the guest's name). If we have two or three bad reports on the same property we will visit incognito to check the problems for ourselves and, sometimes, remove the entry from the next edition of the book.

And finally   If you know a place which would be a good addition to our guides (a B&B, hotel, inn, or other special place in Britain, Spain, France, Ireland, Portugal, Italy, India or Morocco), do let us know. If the property ends up in one of our books because of your recommendation we will send you a free copy. There is a report form at the back of the book or you can e-mail us on: britishholidayhomes@specialplacestostay.com

We hope that you have a fabulous holiday, wherever you go. Don't forget to tell us how you got on.

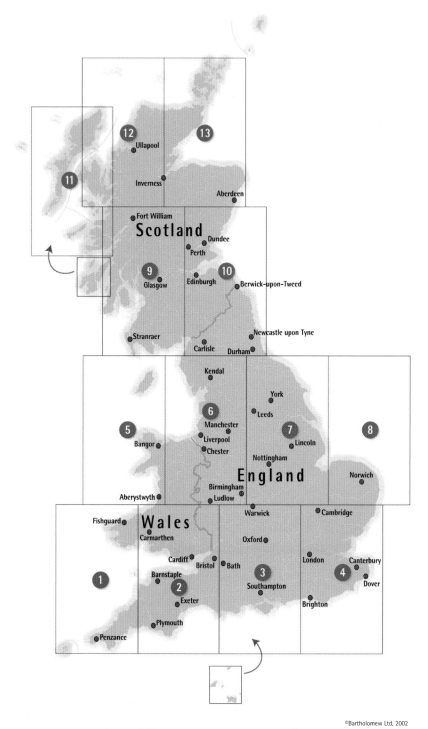

©Bartholomew Ltd, 2002

A guide to our map numbers

Kilmore Broadway
Kilmore Quay

Rosslare

Rosslare

St George's Channel

Cardigan

Newport Bay

Fishguard Bay

A487

93

Newport
Fishguard
PEMBROKESHIRE
Crymych

A40

Llandissilio

*Ramsey
Island*

Haverfordwest

A40

Broad Haven

A4076

92

A477

Milford Haven
Neyland

A478

Pembroke
Dock
Pembroke

Tenby

*Lundy
Island*

C E L T I C   S E A

4

2

Wainhouse Corner

Tintagel

3

A39

Hallworthy

6

5

Camelfor

St Endellion

Padstow

A30

Trenance

Wadebridge

Bodmin

7

Newquay

A38

A392

A391

A390

Perranporth

CORNWALL

St Agnes

A39

St Austell

Portreath

Truro

St Ives

Redruth

Zennor

Camborne

Pendeen

Hayle

Penryn

St Just

Penzance

Falmouth

St Mawes

A394

Helston

Sennen

9

*Isles of
Scilly*

ISLES OF
SCILLY

Land's End

St Keverne

Hugh Town

Lizard Point

Lizard

Map 1

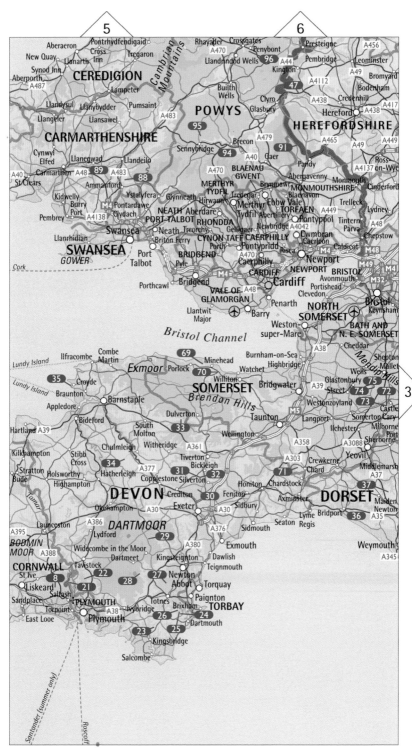

Map 2

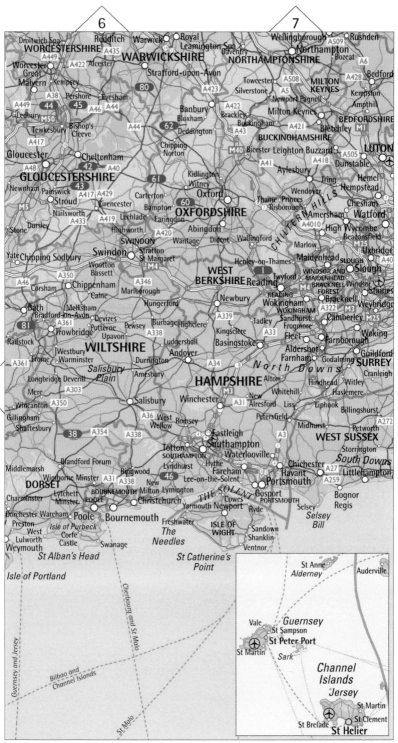

Map 3

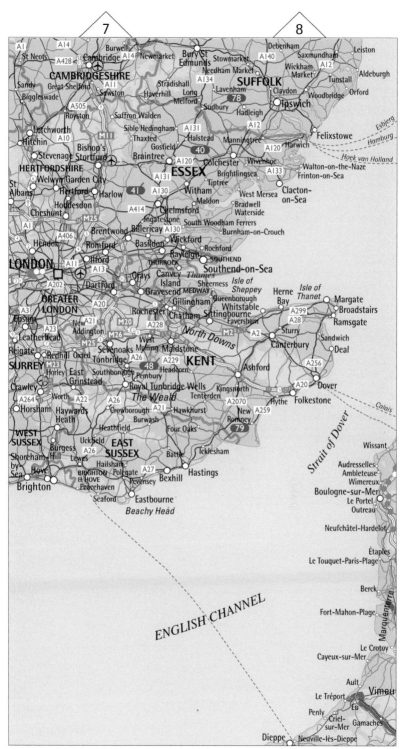

Map 4

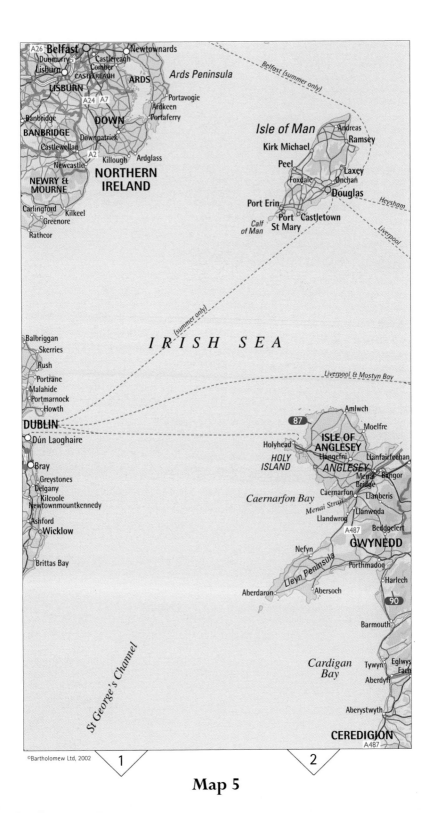

Map 5

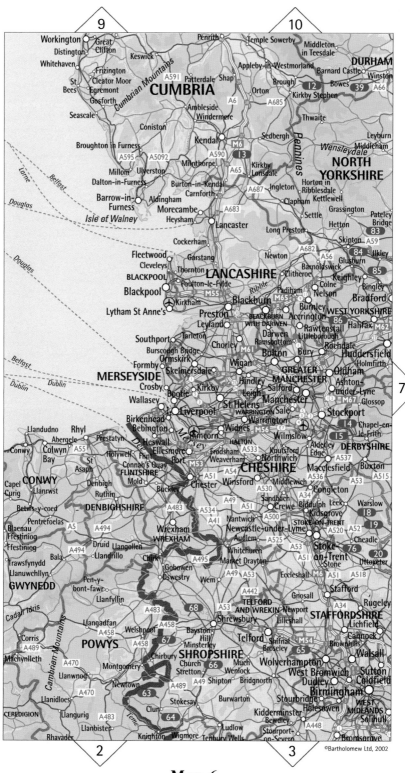

Map 6

©Bartholomew Ltd, 2002

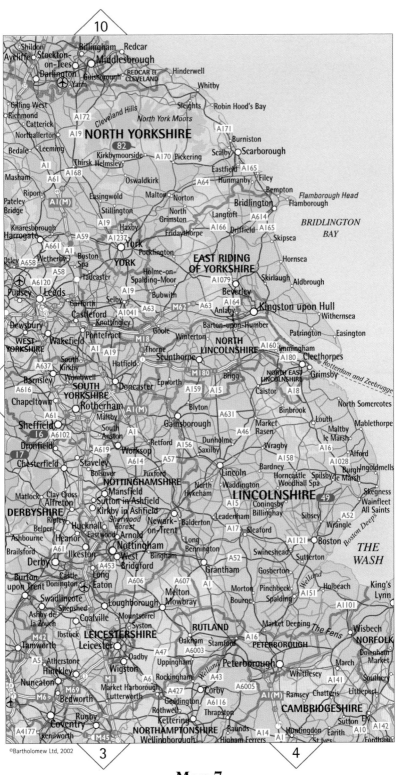

Map 7

©Bartholomew Ltd, 2002

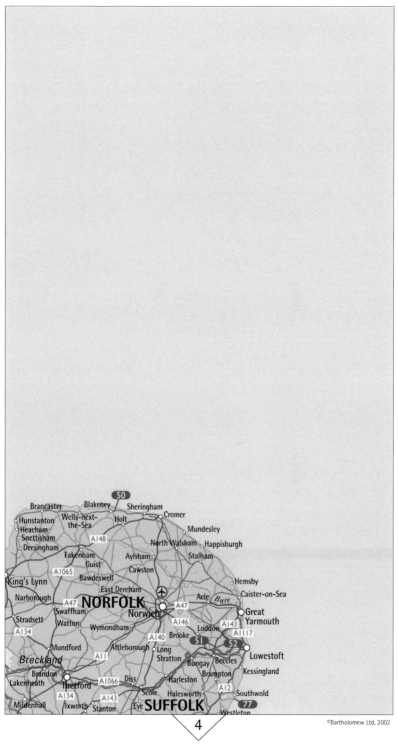

50

Brancaster · Blakeney · Sheringham
Hunstanton · Wells-next-the-Sea · Holt · Cromer
Heacham
Snettisham · A148 · Mundesley
Dersingham · North Walsham · Happisburgh
Fakenham · Aylsham · Stalham
Guist
King's Lynn · A1065 · Cawston
Bawdeswell
East Dereham · Hemsby
Narborough · A47 · NORFOLK · Acle · Bure · Caister-on-Sea
Stradsett · Swaffham · Norwich
Watton · A146 · Loddon · A43 · Great Yarmouth
A134 · Wymondham · Brooke · 51 · A1117
Mundford · A140 · 52
Breckland · A11 · Attleborough · Long Stratton · Lowestoft
Brandon · Bungay · Beccles · Kessingland
Lakenheath · Thetford · A1066 · Diss · Harleston · Brampton
Mildenhall · A134 · A143 · Scole · Halesworth · A12 · Southwold
Ixworth · Stanton · Eye · SUFFOLK · 77
Westleton

4

Map 8

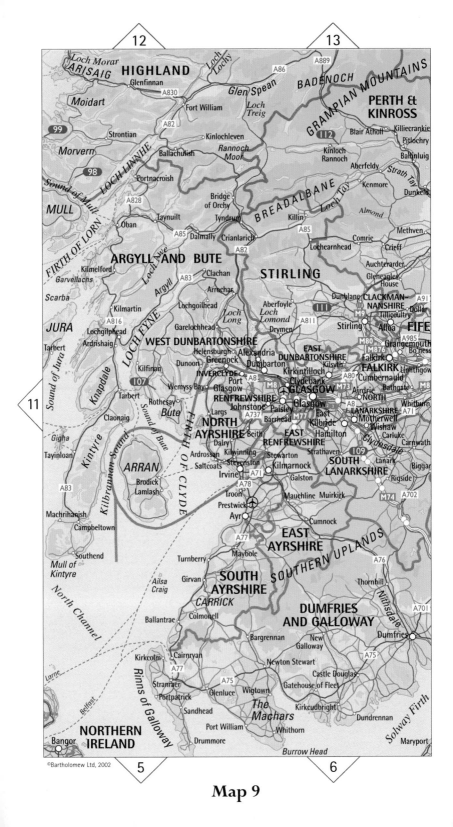

Map 9

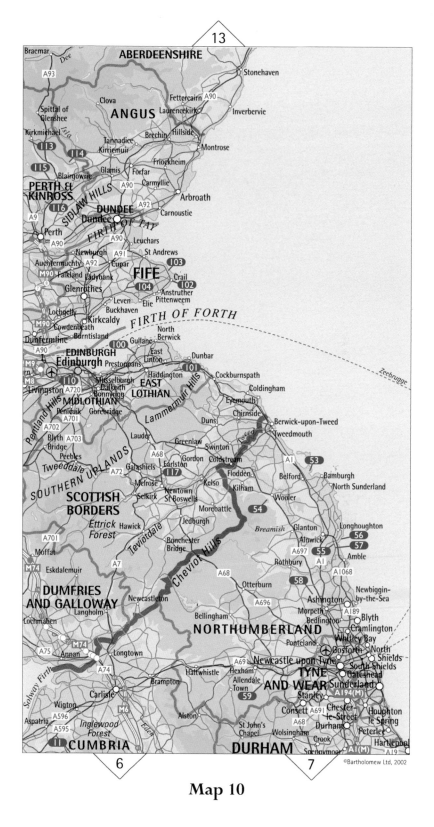

Braemar
Dee
A93
ABERDEENSHIRE
Stonehaven
Clova
Fettercairn
A90
Spittal of
Glenshee
Laurencekirk
Inverbervie
ANGUS
Kirkmichael
Isla
113
114
Tannadice
Brechin
Hillside
Kirriemuir
Montrose
115
Glamis
Forfar
Friockheim
Blairgowrie
Carmyllie
PERTH &
KINROSS
SIDLAW HILLS
A90
A9
116
DUNDEE
Arbroath
Dundee
A92
Carnoustie
Perth
FIRTH OF TAY
A90
Leuchars
A90
Newburgh
A91
St Andrews
Auchtermuchty
A92
Cupar
103
M90
Falkland
Ladybank
FIFE
Crail
Glenrothes
104
Anstruther
102
Lochgelly
Leven
Pittenweem
Cowdenbeath
Buckhaven
Elie
FIRTH OF FORTH
M90
Kirkcaldy
North
Dunfermline
Burntisland
Berwick
Gullane
A90
100
East
EDINBURGH
Prestonpans
Dunbar
Edinburgh
Linton
M9
Haddington
101
Cockburnspath
Musselburgh
M8
EAST
Coldingham
Livingston
A720
Dalkeith
LOTHIAN
Bonnyrigg
Eyemouth
MIDLOTHIAN
Gorebridge
Duns
Chirnside
Penicuik
Lauder
Berwick-upon-Tweed
A701
Blyth
A703
Greenlaw
Tweedmouth
Bridge
Swinton
Peebles
A68
A1
53
Tweeddale
A72
Galashiels
Earlston
Gordon
Coldstream
117
Flodden
Belford
Bamburgh
SOUTHERN UPLANDS
Melrose
Kelso
North Sunderland
SCOTTISH
Selkirk
Newtown
Kilham
Wooler
BORDERS
St Boswells
Morebattle
54
Ettrick
Hawick
Jedburgh
Breamish
Glanton
Longhoughton
Forest
Bonchester
Alnwick
56
A701
Bridge
Cheviot Hills
Rothbury
55
57
Moffat
Teviotdale
A697
A1
Amble
Eskdalemuir
A7
A68
A1068
M74
Otterburn
58
Newbiggin-
DUMFRIES
by-the-Sea
AND GALLOWAY
Newcastleton
A696
Ashington
Morpeth
A189
Blyth
Langholm
Bellingham
A69
Ponteland
Cramlington
Lochmaben
NORTHUMBERLAND
Whitley Bay
M74
Longtown
Gosforth
North
A75
Haltwhistle
Hexham
Newcastle upon Tyne
Shields
Annan
A74
Brampton
Allendale
TYNE
South Shields
Solway Firth
Town
59
AND WEAR
Gateshead
Carlisle
Sunderland
Wigton
M6
Stanley
A194(M)
Aspatria
A596
Alston
Consett
A691
Chester-
Houghton
A595
St John's
A68
le-Street
le Spring
11
Inglewood
Chapel
Wolsingham
Durham
Peterlee
CUMBRIA
Forest
Eden
Crook
Hartlepool
DURHAM
A1(M)
A19
Spennymoor

Zeebrugge

©Bartholomew Ltd, 2002

Map 10

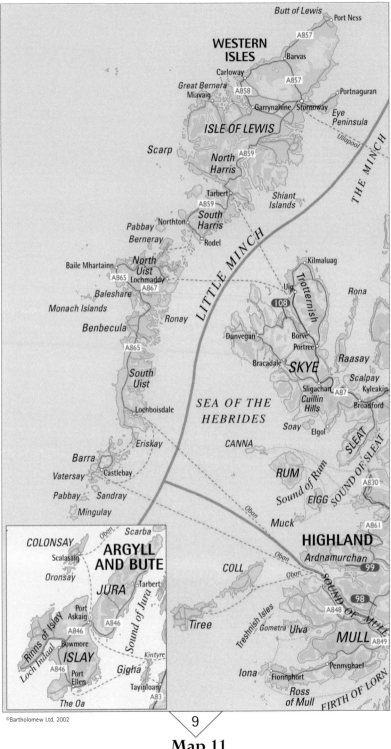

Butt of Lewis   Port Ness

WESTERN ISLES

A857

Barvas

Carloway

A857

Great Bernera   A858

Miavaig

Garrynahine   Stornoway   Portnaguran

Eye Peninsula

ISLE OF LEWIS

Ullapool

Scarp

THE MINCH

North Harris   A859

Tarbert   *Shiant Islands*

A859

South Harris

Pabbay   Northton

Berneray

Rodel

Kilmaluag

Baile Mhartainn

North Uist

A865   Lochmaddy

A867

LITTLE MINCH

Uig   *Trotternish*   *Rona*

108

Baleshare

Monach Islands

Ronay

Dunvegan   Borve

Portree

Bracadale   *SKYE*   *Raasay*

Scalpay

Sligachan   A87   Kyleakin

Cuillin Hills   Broadford

Benbecula

A865

South Uist

Lochboisdale

SEA OF THE HEBRIDES

Soay   Elgol   *SLEAT*

CANNA

SOUND OF SLEAT

Eriskay

Barra

RUM   *Sound of Rum*

A830

Vatersay   Castlebay

Pabbay   Sandray

EIGG

Mingulay

Oban

Muck

A861

COLONSAY   *Oban*   Scarba

Scalasaig

ARGYLL AND BUTE

HIGHLAND

Ardnamurchan

99

Oronsay

JURA   Tarbert

COLL   *Oban*

SOUND OF MULL

98

Port Askaig   A846

A846

Sound of Jura

A848

Rinns of Islay

Bowmore

ISLAY   Kintyre

A846   Port Ellen

Gigha

Tayinloan

A83

The Oa

Treshnish Isles

Gometra   Ulva

MULL   A849

Tiree

Iona   Fionnphort   Pennyghael

Ross of Mull   *FIRTH OF LORN*

Loch Indaal

9

Map 11

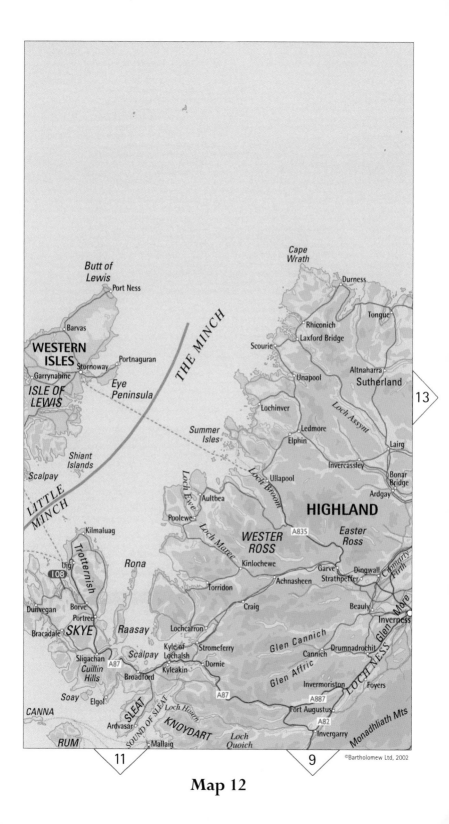

Map 12

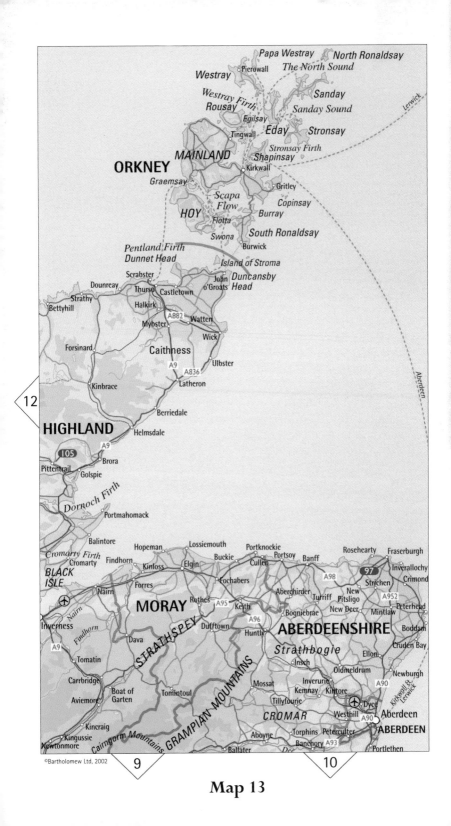

Map 13

Photography by Michael Busselle

ENGLAND

"The really precious things are thought and sight,
not pace."

RUSKIN

Pennycroft
Upper Basildon, Berkshire

Dormered and chimneyed in that comforting Berkshire way, with roses clambering up the porch, the 1905 cottage was originally built for labourers on the Basildon Park estate. You approach via a narrow lane, through wildflower-scattered woods, fields and parkland; below is the Thames Valley, still famed for its wicker baskets, clinker-built boats and dripping oars – the countryside was immortalised in *Wind In The Willows*. Your cottage is cosy, cottagey and comfortable: an open log fire in the sitting room, sofas, armchairs, Colefax & Fowler wallpaper, books and board games galore. The bedrooms are frilly and flowery, charmingly so, two of them with bunk beds and Chiltern views. There's a dining-room with mahogany table and woodburning stove, a shiningly well-equipped kitchen with a table for six and a stocked pantry; bed linen and towels are provided. It is a place to settle into: raspberries and blackcurrants in the garden, lawns all around for picnics and barbecues, fine walks from the door, and Oxford's fabled spires 40 minutes away.

sleeps	6-8.
price	£350-£595.
rooms	4: 1 double; 1 twin; 2 rooms each with double bunk; bath & wc; wc.
closed	Never.

booking details

Chris & Viveka Collingwood

tel	020 8769 2742
fax	020 867 73023
e-mail	info@pennycroft.com
web	www.pennycroft.com

Pa's Cottage
Crackington Haven, Cornwall

This part of Cornwall is known for its surfing beaches, majestic cliffs, coastal path and rock pools ideal for shrimping and crabbing; here you are a bucket's throw from the sea! The thatched longhouse – hundreds of years old, with traditional cob walls of clay and chopped straw – has been divided to made a pair of characterful holiday homes. Pa's Cottage is the larger of the two. Comfy, green-carpeted bedrooms have lots of wonky old rafters, books and sea views; furniture's simple but fine and there's loads of wardrobe space. Downstairs is a fresh and well-equipped kitchen, with smart white china, larder fridge/freezer, yellow daisy curtains and lots of worktop space. Eat at the old pine dining table on Windsor chairs at one end of the big living room – or sink into the sofa by the open fire at the other. There are lots of good eating places in Bude or Boscastle; the Coombe Barton pub 50 yards down the road does family nosh. Be vigilant when you cross the road with children desperate to get to the beach – it gets busy in summer. *Car parking £10 per week in nearby car park.*

sleeps	6.
price	£283–£705.
rooms	3: 1 double; 2 twins; bath & wc; wc.
closed	Never.

booking details

Anna Hardinge

tel	020 7701 9144
e-mail	hania@lovewalk.fsnet.co.uk
web	www.cornwall-online.co.uk/ thatchedcottages

map 1   entry 2

Easterngate Cottage
Crackington Haven, Cornwall

It is wild and beautiful here. The farm, some of it National Trust, has three miles of spectacular coastline, with cliffs rising to 750 feet – the highest in Cornwall – and hauntingly beautiful Strangles Beach where Thomas Hardy walked with Emma. The cottage, which looks down a wooded valley towards Crackington Haven (great for families) has stacks of space. The big, pine-floored living room is comfortably furnished with some antiques, Turkey rugs, a 1950s drinks cabinet, a bookcase full of books… and French windows that lead to a sun-trap terrace with gorgeous valley views: the perfect spot for breakfasts and barbecues. There is also a lawned garden, safe for little ones. Your well-equipped kitchen has green Denby crockery, walk-in larder and large utility room. The double has a big Victorian iron bedstead and valley views; the twin has a minstrel's gallery to the side with an extra bed. The area is a wildlife haven and the biodiversity is impressive: you will see dolphins, buzzards, kestrels, owls, butterflies galore and skylarks ascending. A big, generous place in a fabulous setting – and Trevigue Restaurant to tempt you up the hill.

sleeps	4 + baby.
price	£430–£750.
rooms	2: 1 double with shower & wc; 1 twin, with 1 shower & wc; shower; wc; sofabed on upstairs gallery.
closed	Never.

booking details

	Gayle Crocker
tel	01840 230418
fax	01840 230418
e-mail	trevigue@talk21.com
web	www.trevigue.co.uk

Thatchways

Crackington Haven, Cornwall

The rounded corner windows tell the story of spectacular views – once you've climbed the 58 steps from your car! This 1930s thatched house is loftily situated in the most glorious National Trust land. The huge and homely sitting room has oak floors, an old pine table, comfy sofas, good pictures, rugs and a deep slate hearth. In the kitchen: wooden worktops and slate each side of the Rayburn (there's also a back-up Baby Belling) and a table that seats six. The double bedroom downstairs leads to a bunk room, both overlooking the charming garden; three of the upstairs rooms – a spacious double with iron bedstead, another double and a room with a single bed and a bunkbed – have amazing sea views. Oak doors, a cream shower room downstairs and a green bathroom up are nostalgic reminders of the house's age. Children can have fun exploring the garden with its small rope swing and dens, and there's a sensational spot from which to look out over the beach, hear the crashing of surf below, or sit on a wonderful curved bench to watch the sun set. Crackington Haven has a fine sand-and-surf bay (flagged for safety) and a pub and a beach café. No phone, no TV – but who needs them here?

sleeps	10 + baby.
price	£250-£1,000.
rooms	5: 4 doubles; 1 children's room; bath; shower & wc; wc.
closed	Never.

booking details

	Mark Warby
tel	020 7703 7226
fax	0207 708 4500
e-mail	annkenrick@yahoo.co.uk
web	www.cornwall-online.co.uk/ thatchedcottages

map 1   entry 4

Cornish Tipi Holidays
St Kew, Cornwall

A great idea, born of goodwill and a profound sense of what makes people happy. Lizzie has created a magical, laid-back world of sylvan beauty – 31 tipis of white canvas, lent great swathes of colour by their low-level linings that shut off some light and create atmosphere. The floors are covered with Turkish rugs; there are bed-rolls, North African lanterns, a powerful camping-gaz light, a baby Belling cooker, kitchen box full of utensils, and all you need to start a camp fire outside. You walk to the lovely wooden shower blocks and loos. In fact you walk everywhere once you have arrived; no cars are allowed after unloading. The site is in 16 acres of undulating woodland on the site of an old quarry originally owned by Lizzie's grandfather. Streams and grass pathways meander through and there is a long, beautiful lake where you can swim and catch fish. No concrete, no nasty signs, no noise – just wildlife. There's a pool for toddlers and a barbecue once a week for you all, with live music in the 'big' tipi. Choose your site: side by side with another tipi, on your own or all together. It is a place hand-crafted with love and intelligence.

sleeps	2-6 per tipi.
price	£295-£450 + headage charge at £12 per person; children under 3 exempt.
rooms	Medium sleeps 2 (+ baby); large sleeps up to 6; 2 shower blocks with wc.
closed	November-March.

booking details

	Elizabeth Tom
tel	01208 880781
fax	01208 880487
e-mail	info@cornish-tipi-holidays.co.uk
web	www.cornish-tipi-holidays.co.uk

Rashleigh

Port Gaverne, Cornwall

Here are eight fishermen's cottages round an enclosed courtyard, centrally heated and double glazed. Sleeping six, Rashleigh is the largest, and is all on one floor. These are houses built for fisherfolk to protect against the wild outdoors, so... views are to courtyard not sea. But it would be hard to imagine a more convenient place for a young family to stay: the grassy, sunny courtyard, with outdoor furniture, is totally safe, you are a pebble's throw from rock pools and little cove, and the magical coastal path runs right through the village. Your cottage door opens into a kitchen with sitting and dining area off it: white walls, terracotta twist carpeting and matching sofas, wall lights, cream curtains, beams. The kitchen is compact and well-equipped; bedrooms are carpeted; one looks onto the courtyard, the other two have velux windows up high. Nothing plush, but a very decent place to stay. You are bang opposite the Port Gaverne, once a 17th-century inn, now a stylish hotel serving fresh food in a modern English way, and wonderful Port Isaac is a short puff up the hill. *Laundry shared with other cottages.*

sleeps	6.
price	£343–£567.
rooms	3: 2 double; 1 twin; bath & wc.
closed	Never.

booking details

Mrs Midge Ross

tel	01208 880244
fax	01208 880151
web	www.chycor.co.uk/hotels/port-gaverne

map 1   entry 6

Glynn Barton Cottages
Bodmin, Cornwall

Like the Pied Piper, Andy Orr leads the visiting children away – to collect eggs and meet the donkey, sheep, ducks and rabbits. And there's great planting in progress in the 13 acres of these thoughtfully renovated 18th-century farm buildings, dotted on a hillside with amazing wooded valley views. On the brick terrace or the immaculate lawns children are wonderfully safe, and there's so much to keep them happy: swimming, tennis, table-tennis, games, videos, books. Two huge barbecue areas, one covered, one further up the hill, have picnic tables and long views. Rooms are on the ground floor and blues and sunny yellows prevail. The open plan living rooms have comfy sofas, gas 'woodburners' and exposed beams; the kitchens all you need. Furniture is new pine – tables, dresser, four-poster bed; walls yellow artex, floors fawn-carpeted, bedcovers big check. Bathrooms are spotless. It's possible to take the whole complex and eat together in one of the games rooms – a perfect place for big family gatherings. You are eight miles from the Eden Project, and near surfing-and-sand beaches, too. *There are six cottages in total, for groups of up to 26.*

sleeps	2, 4, 4, 4, 6, 6.
price	£161–£996.
rooms	**Tackroom** 1 double; bath & wc. **Storehouse** 1 double; 1 twin; bath & wc. **Grooms** 1 double; 2 bunks; bath; wc. **Bull Run** 1 double; 1 twin; bath & wc. **Stables** 2 doubles; 1 twin; bath & wc. **Hayloft** 1 double; 2 twins; bath & wc.
closed	Never.

booking details

	Andy & Lucy Orr
tel	01208 821375
fax	01208 821104
e-mail	cottages@glynnbarton.fsnet.co.uk
web	www.glynnbarton.co.uk

Owl Barn
Pillaton, Cornwall

Myrtle from this farm was carried by Queen Victoria in her wedding bouquet; Princess Anne chose white heather from the same source. Two barns and a coach house are being restored, hence the 'before' photograph – watch this space; the newly-hung slates on Owl Barn disguise early 19th-century origins. The heating is geothermal, keeping the place super-snug in winter yet cool in summer – perfect. The living space is open-plan and oak-floored with a mixture of modern leather sofas and antique desks and tables. The predominantly white colour scheme reaches from the porcelain in the kitchen to the goosedown duvets in the light and airy bedrooms. Owl Barn has its own terrace and two lawn areas with tables, chairs and built-in barbecue; the views across the valley to the west are outstanding. Although so close to both coasts, the Eden Project and Cotehele House, this area remains one of Cornwall's undiscovered secrets – deeply peaceful and rich with wild flowers and birdlife, rolling hills and valleys. Guests without a car can be collected from Saltash.

sleeps	6.
price	£500–£1,200.
rooms	3: 2 doubles, with shower & wc, 1 double with bath & wc.
closed	Never.

booking details

Beth & Hugh Bailey

tel	01579 350435
e-mail	kernock.house@amserve.net

map 2   entry 8

Burnewhall House

Nr St Buryan, Cornwall

The big old granite house stands in a wild, windswept place between Lamorna Cove and Land's End: bleak on a foggy day, breathtaking on a fine one. Kenneth, "the most perfect of hosts", does B&B in the main part of the house, you self-cater in the wing; he is hugely welcoming and fun, and an inspired cook, happy to provide printed menus (and Cornish clotted cream!). Your sitting room, a cosy mix of patterned carpeting, old armchairs, new director's chairs and splendid working grate, is special not for its sartorial elegance but for its view: a Victorian bay window frames rolling acres of wheat fields and sea. The kitchen, with cream and green painted floorboards (and handy food mixer) is just off this room, so you can cook while you chat. Biggish bedrooms are soft and easy on the eye; the twin, with washstand in a corner, has the best view. Sip pink gins with Kenneth and guests, walk the grass maze and feel on the edge of the world. Or dream in the herb garden to the side – a private place. A pathway leads to Penberth Cove for swimming (15 minutes), the Logan Rock Inn has good food, St Buryan a brilliant deli. Come for this coast – and for Kenneth.

sleeps	4.
price	£260–£650.
rooms	2: 1 double with shower & wc; 1 twin with shower & wc.
closed	Never.

booking details

	Kenneth Fraser Annand
tel	01736 810650
fax	01736 810650
e-mail	burnewhall@btconnect.com

Chez Wendy
Isle of View, Cornwall

Any decent estate agent would write thus: 'situated in the middle of a lake with unparalleled views of the surrounding countryside, this superb replica executive-dwelling comprises of six well-appointed rooms with every modern convenience. Suitable for the modern executive with little time for DIY efforts, this fine property has been cleverly reduced in size to accommodate the minimalist requirements of people who are busy in the City and need somewhere to escape which requires nothing in the way of maintenance'. Well who are we to disagree? But we should add that it is a perfect place for people with very small children. They can even pick it up and put it down elsewhere on the lake shore. An added feature: it wobbles splendidly in a high wind and may even take you off on an adventure. The interior is plush beyond belief; there are even chandeliers and vanity units. We were keen to include it because it is so unusual. The position is unique, the peace total and the owners endearingly diminutive. And we have to confess that they were able to offer us inducements of an unusual nature. Go, stoop and conquer.

sleeps	0-2 depending on size.
price	Wendy accepts tiny model credit cards.
rooms	6: all too small to get into, but very tastefully decorated.
closed	Whenever the weather dictates.

booking details

Wendy, The Housekeeper

tel	0123456789
fax	9876543210
e-mail	wendy@miniminiminitel.net
web	www.awaywiththetinypeople.con

 map 0   entry 10

Barn Cottage
Bassenthwaite, Cumbria

You can walk to Skiddaw, the third highest hill in the Lakes, from the door; there are few outdoor pleasures that cannot be had from here. The barn was built 250 years ago, and has been converted in the nicest possible way – a handsome slate floor, low-slung old beams, a dresser with plates and cups dangling, a soft blue sofa with colourful cushions and a woodburner for snug nights in. A wooden rocking chair by the window completes the picture and a basket of home-made breads, jams, own free-range eggs and cheese completes the welcome. More homeliness upstairs: fine beams, antique christening robes on white-plastered walls, wooden floors, colourful duvets. Both rooms are smallish, but don't feel cramped. In the bathroom the bath stands free, the walls are panelled and the loo has a high cistern and chain. Lots of old pots, vases and baskets are scattered around in a charming manner. The finest feature of the cottage, however, is the tall protruding window that illuminates the sitting room and lets in the sunset. There's no garden to speak of, but a river runs by across the road and is a good place to sit and reflect.

sleeps	4.
price	£200–£375.
rooms	2: 1 double; 1 twin; bath & wc.
closed	Never.

booking details

Roy & Chris Beaty

tel	01768 776440
web	www.willowbarncottage.co.uk

Stableyard Cottage

Brough, Cumbria

Hope that it rains and you can snuggle in for the day. Your castellated, perpendicular-windowed fantasy cottage – once the stables to the Bennetts' grand castle/folly – is so cosy it's more like a house you've borrowed than a holiday let. In Cumbria's lush and unsung Eden Valley you have glorious views from the living/dining room upstairs – a light and airy room, cosy with carpet, rugs, exposed stone wall and a woodburner flanked by baskets of logs (on the house, of course). In the charming kitchen: rustic white-painted walls, blue wooden cupboards, a boldly-checked blind with cottagey frill, Bridgewater pottery... a lovely, lived-in feel and with a bird's eye view onto the gentle courtyard activity below. Down the carpeted open-tread stairs to bedrooms white-walled and softly lit, and a sparkling white bathroom with huge towels. A garden that captures the afternoon sun, tree-filled acres to roam (two planted for every one cleared), and hosts so considerate they take away your dishes and wash them. They are a delightful pair with young children – bring yours. *Laundry services shared on site.*

sleeps	4.
price	£350–£500.
rooms	2: 1 double; 1 twin; bath & wc.
closed	Never.

booking details

	Wendy & Simon Bennett
tel	01768 341937
e-mail	enquiries@augillcastle.co.uk
web	www.augillcastle.co.uk

map 6   entry 12

Church Brow Cottage

Kirkby Lonsdale, Cumbria

Much of what is best about rural Britain is here: quirky architecture, a terraced garden with a tangle of flowers and a magical view of valley, mountain, river, field and wooded hills. The cottage stands on a steep slope above the River Lune and the garden cascades down the hill to the water's edge. It was built around 1830 for a Dr Pearson as a summerhouse; he was so taken with the beauty of the plot that he diverted a public footpath that ran through it – you'll not be disturbed! Wordsworth immortalized Kirkby Lonsdale and John Ruskin described the view as one of the loveliest he'd seen. Your cottage-in-miniature has three stories, with kitchen (absolutely everything you need) and bathroom on the ground floor; from here you can tip-toe up a steep spiral stone stair to the sitting room, where steps lead down to the formally-planted upper garden terrace – perfect. A spiral stair leads from the sitting room, up to the bedroom under the eaves: a charming and beautifully restful room with pale painted floorboards, old brass bedstead, antique quilt and painted furniture. But why linger? Fix a picnic and a bottle of wine and spend the day by the water's edge. A delicious place.

sleeps	2.
price	£495–£620.
rooms	1 double; bath & wc.
closed	Never.

booking details

	Vivat Trust
tel	0845 090 0194
fax	0845 090 0174
e-mail	enquiries@vivat.org.uk
web	www.vivat.org.uk

The Old House

Whaley Bridge, Derbyshire

Pretty and immaculate – many have described The Old House as "a dream cottage". Farm and outbuildings have been in the family for 200 years and the Broadhursts pour much love and energy into their upkeep. This, the original farmhouse, was built around 1560; three centuries later Charles Wesley, prolific writer of hymns, slept here. Cote Bank Farm is a place where history, atmosphere and peace intertwine, where beautiful mullioned windows contain the original glass; scratched onto one pane, in perfect copybook script: "George Kyrke came to the Coate Bank 1692". Perch on the oak window seat, almost as old, and gaze onto sheep-clad hills. The sitting room is large and lovely with an inglenook hogging one wall (logs provided); a Jacobean table and two Cromwellian chairs sit happily with red rug and emerald sofa. Up the widest-ever stair to the bedroom where rose-coloured drapes soar from antique bedhead to wooden beam, and swags of dried flowers grace white walls. The kitchen is large and superbly equipped. Wake to birdsong with the prospect of breakfast in the undulating garden. Very special. *Cottages (see entry 15) share laundry and games room.*

sleeps	2.
price	£230–£390.
rooms	1 double; bath, shower & wc.
closed	Never.

booking details

	Pamela & Nick Broadhurst
tel	01663 750566
fax	01663 750566
e-mail	cotebank@btinternet.com.
web	www.cotebank.co.uk

map 6   entry 14

Cherry Tree Cottage
Buxworth, Derbyshire

A more idyllic spot for families would be hard to imagine. Pamela is fun, and so thoughtful; Nicholas helps children collect eggs and bottle-feed lambs. When it snows he offers sledges to borrow – they call him "Farmer Nic". Your cottage, the old hay barn, is a warm soft nest: furnishings cosset, the open fire is stocked with logs and the gingham-curtained kitchen with every modern comfort (dishwasher included); in the bathroom are stacks of towels. The old barn doorway is your studio window that pulls the sunlight in. Bedrooms with velux windows are carpeted and cosy; stencils and flowery fabrics abound, so do crooked beams. Dining room and little patio face south; from your Yorkstoned outdoor spot you overlook the circular, tree-fringed farmyard with hills and valley beyond. In the evenings the ping-pong room next door comes into its own, stocked with books, TV, toys and exercise bike – not that you'll need it with all those walks from the door. A sublime setting at the end of a quiet country lane, and just a mile from Chinley village, with several eating places. Perfect. *Cottages (see entry 14) share laundry and games room.*

sleeps	4-6.
price	£230-£600.
rooms	1 double; 1 twin, 1 room with bunks; bath & wc; shower & wc.
closed	Never.

booking details

Pamela & Nick Broadhurst

tel	01663 750566
fax	01663 750566
e-mail	cotebank@btinternet.com.
web	www.cotebank.co.uk

North Lees Hall

Hathersage, Derbyshire

The romance of the tower fired Charlotte Brontë who placed Jane Eyre's Mr Rochester here, in the fictional Thornfield Hall. The crenellated roof is an Elizabethan affectation, but those mullioned windows – imagine the light within. It is right on a walking path, with a steady trickle of walkers, and sheep; the views are stupendous from every room. First, the Lower Apartment: a large and lovely bedroom with theatrically draped four-poster, stone fireplace, tapestry drapes, painted panelled walls, sofa and painting of Elizabeth I. The kitchen and bathroom are plain but pleasing, the former with a long oak table and benches. Up an astonishing elm spiral stair (children beware) to the Upper Apartment: a vast sitting room with elaborate plaster ceiling, period furniture, heavy oak doors, a log-burning stove. The kitchen is like the one below, yet feels bigger. The master room has a four-poster, fine white bed linen and a huge, elaborate sofa with carved arms. The other bedroom is smaller, cosier, and there's a small roof terrace with decking. There is a small outdoor space for the Lower Apartment or stroll instead into the bucolic stage-set that is North Lees.

sleeps	**Upper** 4 + 1 baby. **Lower** 2 + 1 baby.
price	**Upper** £560–£725. **Lower** £435–£555.
rooms	**Upper** 2 doubles; bath & wc. **Lower** 1 double; bath & wc.
closed	May be closed for repairs during parts of 2003 – phone for details.

booking details

	Vivat Trust
tel	0845 090 0914
fax	0845 090 0174
e-mail	enquiries@vivat.org.uk
web	www.vivat.org.uk

map 7   entry 16

Garden Cottage
Cressbrook, Derbyshire

What's truly special here are the grounds of the Hall and the fact that Cressbrook is almost plumb in the centre of the Peak District National Park. Built for the mill owner circa 1835, the mansion looks over a dramatic limestone gorge carved out by the River Wye; the elegant gardens, open for viewing in summer, have been recently restored to their original design. Garden Cottage – which opens onto the large conservatory and orangery – is in fact a split-level conversion of the original library, overlooking the garden and majestic green hill beyond. The sitting/dining room has a handsome, marble fireplace, fitted carpet and comfortable three-piece suite. The compact fitted kitchen is no-frills-functional with most things you need. Bedrooms either side of the bathroom have velux and dormer windows; beds are decked in pale and floral fabrics. Two more bedrooms are on the lower level. With that wonderful Derbyshire countryside all around the choice of walks is limitless; Monsal Dale, with its river, waterfall and viaduct, is a 20-minute stroll along the valley. B&B is offered in the hall. *Laundry/games room/sauna in Hall, shared with other self-catering cottages.*

sleeps	4-7.
price	£225-£750.
rooms	4: 1 double; 2 twins; 1 single; bath & wc.
closed	Christmas & New Year.

booking details

Bobby & Len Hull-Bailey

tel	01298 871289
fax	01298 871845
e-mail	stay@cressbrookhall.co.uk
web	www.cressbrookhall.co.uk

Church Farm Cottage

Nr Alstonefield, Derbyshire

You can give a helping hand at lambing or harvest time – animal lovers, environmentalists and children will adore this place. The cottage originally formed part of the Grade II-listed farmhouse; the family have farmed here since time immemorial and one building is listed in the Domesday Book. Managed organically, the summer meadows brim with wild flowers and herbs, and the farmyard – where sheep have names – rivals Old MacDonald's with all the dogs, cats, hens, cows and sheep. Sue's delightful touch extends inside to the shining copper and brass, the fresh flowers and the examples of her own handiwork: stencils and embroidery. A red sofa and chairs surround the original yet super-efficient range. Floral curtains are in keeping with the cottagey mood, as are iron latches on the green kitchen cupboards and the traditional white china sink. The attic twin has delightful yellow *toile de Jouy* bedheads and matching curtains. Add a small, secure cottage garden and dreamy views and you have a rural idyll. *Pets by arrangement.*

sleeps	4.
price	£260–£507.
rooms	2: 1 double; 1 twin; bath & wc; shower & wc.
closed	Never.

booking details

	Sue Fowler
tel	01335 310243
fax	01335 310243
e-mail	sue@fowler89.fsnet.co.uk
web	www.dovedalecottages.co.uk

map 6   entry 18

The Groom's Quarters

Hall Lane, Wootton, Derbyshire

The conversion – from groom's home and tack room to holiday hideaway for six – is superb. Quarry tiles, stone, exposed brickwork, original tack room features, chunky beams and doors form a refreshingly rustic backdrop to bold colours, huge tapestry-fabric sofas, sparkling bathrooms and cast-iron bed... not a trace of fussiness in sight. The kitchen is brand new, a contemporary mix of stainless steel, white cupboards and wood, with both oven and oil-fired range – revel in the simplicity of it all. You'll sleep the sleep of the righteous in the big bedrooms with their six-foot beds and lofty A-frame ceilings. The exterior woodwork is that particularly English grey-green; courtyard cobbles and original stables remain (bring your own horse!). Then there's Ann who creates the caring, happy environment and proffers home-baked cake on arrival. She can tell you heaps about the area and the Wootton estate, for centuries the Davenport family seat. Gather round the woodburner to celebrate your discovery of this place, then head off to explore the rural charms of the Peak District. And market towns Ashbourne and Leek will delight the dedicated shopper.

sleeps	6-8.
price	£295-£695.
rooms	3: 1 double; 1 master double with sofabed; 1 twin; bath, shower & wc.
closed	Never.

booking details

Ray & Ann Thompson

tel	01335 324549
e-mail	thompson.wootton@virgin.net
web	freespace.virgin.net/thompson.wootton

Stable Wing
Snelston, Derbyshire

This was once the groom's flat over the stables of an interestingly narrow 1840s house designed by Cottingham. Tall cylindrical brick chimneys – his architectural trade mark – are on display all over this estate village on the edge of the Derbyshire Peaks. Your well-furnished flat is perfectly suited to a couple, though there is actually room for four. The kitchen is tiny but beautifully kitted out with good china and everything you could hope for. The good-sized double bedroom with pretty Jane Churchill curtains has a king-size bed with duvet and white linen sheets; the twin is small. In the sitting room, comfortable sofa and armchairs, oriental rugs, a small collection of books and watercolours, and an open log fire; a little oak gate-leg table in the corner opens up for meals. Ashbourne, a 10-minute drive, has good restaurants, fine antique shops, a farmers' market and a famous gingerbread shop. The Derbyshire scenery is wonderful and scattered with famous houses. Space apart, this is a highly civilised base in a really lovely part of the world – and one too frequently overlooked.

sleeps	2-4.
price	£350-£400.
rooms	2: 1 double; 1 twin; bath & wc.
closed	Christmas & New Year.

booking details

	Edmund & Sue Jarvis
tel	01335 324510
fax	01335 324113
e-mail	s-jarvis@tiscali.co.uk

map 6   entry 20

South Hooe Mine
Bere Alston, Devon

Lead and silver were the attractions 150 years ago of this steep wooded hillside overlooking the glittering estuary; redolent of its history, the Georgian mining captain's house feels solid and well lived in. Outside, slate-hung walls and old slate floors in the kitchen and hall. Inside, well-loved furnishings have their stories to tell: pictures and portraits, family antiques and country pine, oriental rugs, a dresser graced with antique china in white and blue. There's plenty of seating at dining and kitchen tables, and a log fire and woodburner to keep you cosy. Bedrooms – soft pine, white linen – are as lovely as their river views; all but one have basins and there are enough bathrooms for comfort. French windows open to a sheltered garden where campion, roses and ox-eye daisies grow: a heavenly spot for *al fresco* meals. Martha the donkey helps out with the mowing. The sailing is magnificent and there's a deep-water mooring below the house, available by arrangement. All this and views to mesmerise: wading birds, scudding boats and ever-changing light. *Families with young children beware the old mine shaft and fast-flowing tidal river.*

sleeps	9-10.
price	£850.
rooms	6: 1 double with bath & wc; 1 twin & 1 single with bath & wc; 2 doubles; 1 single; shower and wc.
closed	Let for self-catering in July & August. Rest of year B&B.

booking details

	Trish Dugmore
tel	01822 840329

Tower Cottage
Buckland Abbey, Devon

Cistercian monks may have meditated under the ancient apple tree in the garden and certainly Sir Francis Drake will have climbed to the top of the medieval tower next door. Tranquillity reigns in this atmospheric place: 16 acres of gardens and fields surrounded by National Trust land to walk in. While not luxurious – the monks can rest in peace – your cottage is homely, solid and comfortable with white walls, chunky armchairs, good pictures, damask and crewelwork curtains, logs in the open fire. The dining room has an array of blue and white china on its pine dresser; an arch leads to the well-equipped kitchen. Bedrooms are traditional and flowery – one with an antique double bed – and have views of the courtyard. Sarah's walled garden is exceptionally lovely – there's a bench from which to enjoy it all – and occasionally opens under the National Gardens Scheme. She also grows organic veg with plenty to spare for guests. The Abbey is open to the public (NT) but the cottage stands in a private courtyard. Steps at the back lead up past the herbs – pick them at your leisure – to the garden and tennis court. A deeply restful place. *Bed linen £8 p.p. per week.*

sleeps	5.
price	£300–£480.
rooms	3: 1 double; 1 twin; 1 single; bath, shower & wc.
closed	Never.

booking details

	Mrs Sarah Stone
tel	01822 853285
fax	01822 853626
e-mail	sarah.stone@cider-house.co.uk

map 2   entry 22

Top Barn

East Allington, Devon

Lush, rolling Devon countryside is the perfect setting for the luxury of this newly converted medieval stone barn. Light from the glassed-in south wall fills the sitting/dining room, furnished with deep, burnt-orange sofas, pale carpet and cream walls. Tall French windows open onto a large terrace with table and barbecue, which in turn leads to a half acre of lawn, a climbing frame, apple trees and meadows. A galley-style kitchen off the main room is small but ergonomic, spotlessly clean and easy to use with its matching yellow gadgets. Upstairs, the two carpeted bedrooms are also light and airy with beams, vaulted ceilings and muslin curtains; from the comfort of your king-size bed, gaze down the sweep of the valley. Bath and shower rooms are spick and span. Set in an old cider orchard, your holiday retreat is completely private. Books and games are to hand, as is a welcome hamper of provisions – including the Frosts' own superb Grimpstonleigh apple juice and cider.

sleeps	4 + baby.
price	£300-£575.
rooms	2: 1 double with shower & wc; 1 twin with bath & wc.
closed	Christmas-New Year.

booking details

Petrina & Kevin Frost

tel	01548 521258
fax	01548 521258
e-mail	grimpstonleigh@ukgateway.net
web	www.grimpstonleigh.com

Little Coombe Cottage

Dittisham, Devon

An avenue of young horse chestnut trees leads steeply down the wooded valley to the secluded one-storey cottage with gardens and ponds. Honeysuckle graces the pillars of the porch; a beamy, open plan sitting and dining room sit on the other side. Hops decorate the stone chimneypiece above the woodburner, Crown & Derby china sits prettily on the antique dresser, the coffee table and fabrics strike an Indian note, and French windows open onto decking with teak table and chairs and lush views down garden and valley. A gleaming woodblock floor carries through to the kitchen, immaculate with cream units, white china, dishwasher. Bedrooms are comfortably furnished, one with a lovely new four-poster with all the trimmings and a smart tub chair; both have French windows onto the decking. All is double-glazed and warm and cosy – good for out of season breaks. You are close to beautiful Dittisham with pubs and store; take the ferry to Dartmouth and walk back along the footpath on the opposite bank of the river. Birdsong in the garden, exotic geese and wildfowl on the ponds, and the friendly Unitts next door. Perfect.

sleeps	4.
price	£230–£495.
rooms	2: 1 double with bath & wc; 1 twin with shower & wc.
closed	Never.

booking details

	Phil & Ann Unitt
tel	01803 722599
fax	01803 722599

map 2   entry 24

Fingals Barn

Dittisham, Devon

When we began to put this book together, we were looking for just this sort of Special Place – unusual, fun, a little bit quirky, wonderfully relaxed. Lying in a rolling valley half a mile from the River Dart, the Barn adjoins Richard's famous Fingals Hotel so everything you need is on the spot – pool, snooker, tennis, croquet and a restaurant that specialises in fresh, French cooking and plenty of fish. The oak-framed Barn was constructed in 1988; reached from an outside stair, the huge open space has massive beams and floor-to-ceiling windows that look onto a grass tennis court and carefully tended garden (shared with hotel guests). Deliciously comfortable sofas, an oriental rug and a rocking horse on a polished oak floor, interesting pictures and wooden birds perched on beams. The functional open plan kitchen is at one end, and the main bedroom, with pine bed and Indian throw, sloping roof and skylight windows, on the other side of a sliding Japanese screen. There's a second, much smaller bedroom just right for children and a marvellous bathroom with a proper green-footed roll-top bath. *Pets welcome by arrangement.*

sleeps	4.
price	£300–£700.
rooms	2: 1 double; 1 twin with wc; bath & wc.
closed	Never.

booking details

Richard Johnston &
Sheila Macdonald

tel	01803 722398
fax	01803 722401
e-mail	richard@fingals.co.uk
web	www.fingals.co.uk

North Barn

Cornworthy, Devon

The river laps at the edge of your bed and you bathe in light. Or so it seems, with nothing but water and sky visible through the great glass-and-timber doors at the end of the big open room that is North Barn. No photo can do it justice, for your first arrival is a breath-stopping moment. It is awash with light and colour, gay with the easy good humour of Pedro and Jilly. He is an architect and she an artist, both of them gifted with a rare ability to bring unfettered imagination to bear on any space. Cook in a galley kitchen (well-equipped), sleep on a platform, curtained for privacy. Slop about on the big wooden deck, with nothing but a sliver of greenery 'twixt you and the river. Or lie in bed all day and gaze at the Dart and its bobbing boats. It is sublime in summer and cosy in winter, with a woodburning stove, music and sofas. The area is riddled with 'attractions' but you may not want to abandon this place. Or you may wait for low tide and pick your way along the foreshore to the restaurant/pub at Tuckenhay. Sybaritically comfortable for two, easy with a child in the single bed.

sleeps	2-4.
price	£275-£425.
rooms	1: 1 double; 1 single; bath & wc; sofabed in living room.
closed	Never.

booking details

	Pedro & Jilly Sutton
tel	01803 865084
fax	01803 722584

map 2   entry 26

Coach House
Staverton, Devon

Under the carved medieval beam where bats roost, into the comfortably furnished rooms of the mellow-stoned coach house of 1735. Your Georgian home is one of several on the estate of Kingston House, a majestic country-house hotel managed by thoughtful hosts. This is quite a plus as you can breakfast in the big house or be seduced by the 'moveable feasts' – home-cooked, home-produced meals brought to your door. The Coach House's high-ceilinged lower floor is open plan and divided by an arch. Rustic whitewashed walls and turquoise carpet in the sitting room, cottagey soft furnishings and woodburner; and an all-singing, all-dancing kitchen with traditional pine dresser and everything you could possibly need from dishwasher to garlic press. Tread the fine wooden stair to a bedroom resplendent with draped four-poster, Percale linen and wild Dartmoor views; a pretty twin; bathrooms with the thickest towels we've seen. Swallows nest under the eaves, there are two pubs to walk to, and acres of formal garden and paddocks to roam. You can even hire a rigged 57-foot motor ketch for the day.

sleeps	4 + baby.
price	£336–£721.
rooms	2: 1 double with shower & wc; 1 twin; bath & wc.
closed	Occasionally.

booking details

	Michael & Elizabeth Corfield
tel	01803 762235
fax	01803 762444
e–mail	info@kingston-estate.co.uk
web	www.kingston-estate.co.uk

Meadow Barn
Michelcombe, Devon

Ducks, goats and chickens range the cobbled courtyard, pony and trap rides can be arranged... step back a hundred years in this enchanting corner of Devon. Down-to-earth, hard-working Judy has taken enormous care to preserve the feeling and appearance of the old barn's exterior while providing the best of modern delights inside. Through the neo-medieval, solid oak front door and into fresh white rooms with beams of limed oak and sills of sycamore. The simply furnished upstairs sitting room has warm red sofas and a woodburning stove. Applewood grown in the Hendersons' orchard has created kitchen cabinets, stylishly topped with slate; the floor is terracotta. More applewood in the cosy twin, while the main bedroom, overlooking the duck pond, has a handmade oak bed and a sweet little dressing room where clothes hang from a hazel bough. The beautifully tended vegetable garden is entirely organic, the spreading oak has a swing, the stream a pretty bridge and the 23 acres of meadow and woodland are fenced in chestnut. It would have been easy to make Meadow Barn chocolate-boxy, but it isn't. It's perfect.

sleeps	4 + baby.
price	£276–£486.
rooms	2: 1 double; 1 twin; bath & wc.
closed	October – end of April.

booking details

Judy Henderson
tel   01364 631461
e-mail   judy@dodbrooke.freeserve.co.uk
web   www.dodbrookefarm.com

map 2   entry 28

The Barn

Long Lane, Devon

Difficult not to use the word 'hideaway'. With the moors, woodlands and fields all around it does feel like a place to hide. The setting is magical, secluded and entirely peaceful; sit and watch the sun go down from your little terraced garden. Hugh and Liza, who also do B&B in the main house, are the kindest people – available to help without intruding. They also grow their own vegetables organically, so, in season, you'll be able to buy from them. They have converted the old farm-implement barn with solid good taste and typical lack of pretension: pine floors and good, modern rugs, a corner kitchen cleverly fitted out, and maximum use of space. There's a Rayburn for winter warmth, a wicker sofa and a double futon to sprawl on and gorgeous views to the moors. The bathroom is cork-tiled, the double bed is king-sized, a brocade curtain hugs the door for cosiness on winter nights, and the bedspread comes from Anouki – an Indian touch. The furniture is modern pine, but just right for this place. The water comes from the spring – a final seductive touch.

sleeps	2-3.
price	£175-£280.
rooms	1: 1 double & sofabed; 1 separate single bunk space; bath & wc.
closed	Very occasionally.

booking details

Liza & Hugh Dagnall

tel	01647 221389
fax	01647 221389
e-mail	easdondown@btopenworld.com

Heathfield Barn

Thorverton, Devon

Heathfield Barn would be a little slice of heaven for city couples making a weekend escape; ideal too for those in a larger group who might like extra space in the studio next door. The Jehus – charming, thoughtful (the welcome pack includes wine and delicious locally-made crisps), multi-lingual – have converted the weatherboarded barn into a Special Place with a contemporary feel: wide-planked oak floors, fresh white walls, reclaimed pitch pine. Bedrooms are beautifully furnished with goose down duvets, good linen and the odd antique; oak and marble and attractive lighting make for excellent bathrooms. Next to the living room is an open plan kitchen, immaculately equipped, of course, with dishwasher, and above, a large mezzanine and minstrel gallery – fun for children – with fabulous roof beams. You have the additional luxury of a woodburning stove for chilly nights; central heating is included. Outside, ping-pong, darts, croquet, even a large trampoline... and wonderful long views beyond apple trees to farmland. You are off the quietest of country lanes in a little-spoiled corner of Devon – good biking country yet 15 minutes from Exeter.

sleeps	6-8.
price	£250-£890.
rooms	3: 1 double with bath & wc; 1 twin with bath & wc; mezzanine with 2 futons & double sofabed; 1 studio flat with sofabed, galley kitchen & shower & wc..
closed	Never.

booking details

	Mrs Mary Jehu
tel	01392 841941
fax	01392 841438
e-mail	su6003@eclipse.co.uk
web	www.heathfieldfarm.net

 map 2   entry 30

Park Wing
Fursdon Cadbury, Devon

A glorious estate above the Exe Valley and Exeter, owned for centuries by the Fursdons and benefitting hugely from their custody. They love the 700 acres, woods, pastures, parkland and house, and share them easily – with you and the public, who, on special days, come to visit. Your quarters are generously furnished and huge, reached via a little cobbled courtyard and a grand oak stair. The sitting room once formed part of a medieval Great Hall; it is deliciously elegant, homely too, with sofas, bookcases and open fire, seagrass floors, coral walls and tall windows with vistas of parkland and Dartmoor – you could sit and gaze for ever. More views from the kitchen; yellow and bluey-green, it has a New England feel. The main bedroom is big and light, with king-size bed, comfy little sofa and those views; the twins are pale and serene, and overlook garden and dovecote, complete with doves. Catriona presides warmly over this safe and peaceful haven, and is a fascinating source of knowledge on the history and the fluctuating fortunes of the place. She also tends a heavenly walled garden. *Garden Wing also available (entry 31).*

sleeps	6.
price	£430–£650.
rooms	3: 1 double; 2 twins; bath; wc.
closed	Never.

booking details

Mrs Catriona Fursdon

tel	01392 860860
fax	01392 860126
e-mail	catriona@fursdon.co.uk
web	www.fursdon.co.uk

Garden Wing

Fursdon Cadbury, Devon

Garden Wing has a different feel to that of Park Wing: more cottage than country house, still stylish in the nicest possible way. Up the oak stairs, past rich tapestries on the wall, into the 18th-century apartment – you will be charmed. The panelled sitting room – once the family school room – is painted perfect Farrow & Ball green-grey, and is cosy with coral sofa and checked cushions, books, antiques and open fire. Steps lead down through a rose-covered arch into the lovely garden. The Shaker-style kitchen is yellow and white, high-ceilinged, beautifully equipped; bedrooms as delightful: a big double with elegant Georgian doorway and garden views, and a tiny single. The only noise to disturb the peace of this unspoiled part of Devon is birdsong and the cooing of doves. It's wonderful for children: swings, football and paddocks with Shetland ponies and sheep, a barbecue for warm nights. There's grass tennis too, and farm trails are in the pipeline. Village pubs (two with good food), shops and farm shop are two miles off, Exeter ten. And then there's Catriona, who so clearly enjoys looking after her guests. *Park Wing also available (entry 32).*

sleeps	3.
price	£260-£450.
rooms	2: 1 double; 1 single; bath & wc.
closed	Never.

booking details

Mrs Catriona Fursdon

tel	01392 860860
fax	01392 860126
e-mail	catriona@fursdon.co.uk
web	www.fursdon.co.uk

map 2   entry 32

Dunsley Mill Barn
West Anstey, Devon

There are 30 secluded acres with a small river gurgling through the middle of it all – the barn was once a mill. Just next door is Exmoor National Park with its red deer and hundreds of miles of walks. It is also one of England's quietest areas. Your holiday house can defy all the elements that the Moor can throw at it: double-glazed and centrally heated and outrageously comfortable. There's a downstairs bathroom and splendid, beamed open-plan sitting room with a dining area and oak-cupboarded kitchen, all carpeted in plain green cord – straightforward and traditional. The three bedrooms have padded dralon headboards and padded flowery bedcovers, floral curtains and simple rattan-effect furniture – nothing unusual but solidly comfortable. Helen is immensely friendly and kind; kind, too, to your dogs who are welcome to live in the hall of the barn. You have a little garden at the back and your own river frontage. It is kempt and cut, neat and pretty – and there is trout fishing nearby.

sleeps	6 + baby.
price	£250–£500.
rooms	3: 2 doubles; 1 twin; 2 baths, showers & wcs.
closed	Occasionally.

booking details

	Helen Sparrow
tel	01398 341374
fax	01398 341374
web	www.dunsleymill.co.uk

Horry Mill

Hollocombe, Devon

Pied fly-catchers, a babbling brook, 20 acres of natural woodland, wild flowers, ducks, chickens, guinea fowl – rural bliss. Mobile phones don't work and television reception is a bit dodgy: what a place for the great escape. This was once a miller's cottage, destroyed by fire in the 18th century, then rebuilt using the old beams and timbers. Sonia has accentuated the original features – the big fireplace in the beamed sitting room, the wide oak stairs, the gleaming floor boards in the bedrooms – and added good solid cottage furniture, lots of games and books, an old iron bedstead with crisp white linen, nice china and a pretty window seat overlooking the cottage garden. She even leaves the Rayburn lit throughout the year – unless it's a hot summer. Milk and newspapers can be delivered, and when Sonia's not looking after their cows, she will do all your shopping for you, so you can put the car in mothballs. She and Simon, who live in the Millhouse a little way away, are continuously improving Horry Mill. You'll love Simon's *pièce de résistance*: a beautiful, wooden thatched summer house a step from your door.

sleeps	6.
price	£245–£480.
rooms	3: 2 doubles; 1 twin; bath & wc; shower.
closed	Never.

booking details

	Sonia & Simon Hodgson
tel	01769 520266
e-mail	horrymill@aol.com
web	www.horrymill.com

map 2   entry 34

Oyster Falls
Croyde, Devon

Perfect for serious surfers and bucket-and-spaders alike. Don't be put off by the rather ordinary looks: this extraordinary bungalow perches alone on a headland overlooking the expanse of Croyde Bay, with Baggy Point and Lundy Island in the distance. It takes its name from the rocks visible in the bay; once a simple beach hut, it was enlarged in the 50s and 60s into a comfortable refuge. Wake to the sound of surf breaking below. Bedrooms are simple and well-furnished with good big wardrobes; the bathroom is smart and spotless. The good-sized sitting/dining room has some nice bits of furniture and there's also a separate, small, French-windowed snug if you feel like a change of scene. Wherever you are, your eye is drawn to the views. It's great for children too. The clean, sandy beaches patrolled by coast guards are pretty safe but do keep an eye on the tides. If you can tear yourself away, there are superb coastal walks, golf courses and gardens to visit and Lundy, a day trip by boat. Croyde – and Georgeham nearby – are picture-postcard villages of thatch and cream teas. A super place.

sleeps	6 + baby.
price	£485–£868.
rooms	3: 1 double; 2 twins; bath & wc; wc.
closed	October–March.

booking details

	Mrs R. W. A. Hare
tel	01271 345039
fax	01271 345039
e–mail	oysterfalls@humesfarm.co.uk
web	www.oysterfalls.co.uk

The Chantry
Bridport, Dorset

Enchanting! Dating from 1300, the earliest secular building in Bridport may have been a primitive lighthouse or toll point; later, when it was a priests' house, masses were sung here: in the main bedroom there's a charming 'piscina' (stone basin) in the alcove. It is a privilege to stay in such a place. Your sitting room, simple, restful, is dominated by a glorious 16th-century stone fireplace, fragments of 17th-century paintings embellish two walls, the kitchen (streamlined, beautiful) is recessed into a historic chimneypiece. Intriguing stonework is complemented by sumptuous textiles, limewashed walls and imaginative use of driftwood, pebbles, sisal and cane. And in what style you sleep: a magnificent master bedroom (with woodburner) to unleash your imagination and enrich your dreams. Up excitingly narrow stairs to the one-time pigeon loft: two bedrooms, one big, one tiny, both charming. You are on a busy road and views are urban but the market town setting will please many – Bridport is full of idiosyncratic shops and unexpected corners.

sleeps	5 + 1 baby.
price	£560-£725.
rooms	3: 1 double; 1 twin, 1 single; bath & wc; shower & wc.
closed	Never.

booking details

	Vivat Trust
tel	0845 090 0194
fax	0845 090 0174
e-mail	enquiries@vivat.org.uk
web	www.vivat.org.uk

map 2   entry 36

Old Gaol Cottage

Cerne Abbas, Dorset

This is Cerne Abbas's Victorian police station – although no-one has been detained at Her Majesty's pleasure since the turn of the century. You can still see the iron-barred cell windows – the American owners, have the original key – but the old cop shop has been transformed into a very fine place to stay. The kitchen is state-of-the-art with a brand new electric range, top-notch utensils and tableware, all the latest gadgets. A touch of the Orient here too: in the sitting and dining rooms, a fine Chinese cabinet and willow-pattern plates. The master bedroom has a sumptuous, queen-size, lace-canopied four-poster, lots of cupboard space, and hunting prints in gilt frames; the original wrought iron windows are softened with Jane Churchill fabrics. The second bedroom also has two five-foot double beds; the bathroom is new, spotless, white. Cerne Abbas is best known for its Giant which was carved into the chalk hillside more than 2,000 years ago; today there's a good local shop and three pubs that serve food – one next door. A stylish Dorset base – our inspector loved it.

sleeps	4-6.
price	£300-£500.
rooms	2: 1 double; 1 family room (2 doubles); bath & wc.
closed	Never.

booking details

	Nicky Willis
tel	01300 341659
fax	01300 341699
e-mail	nickywillis@tesco.net

The Smithy

Fanners Yard, Compton Abbas, Dorset

When Tim and Lucy first explored this Victorian forge across the yard from their house they found the blacksmith's tools exactly where he'd left them. Seventy years on they have restored the building with a meticulous and sensitive eye. Bellows, anvils, pincers and hammers from the smithy's days complement the bare stone, brick, coir matting and ancient roof timbers of the sitting room – warm and cosy with a woodburning stove. The kitchen is small but has all the bits and pieces you need; go through to an immaculately pretty bathroom. Up six steps and you're into the pretty gallery bedroom, with folksy painted furniture, iron bedstead and crisp white cotton sheets. There's a marvellous feeling of tranquillity and solitude here in this Area of Outstanding Natural Beauty where butterflies flutter in fields of rare wild flowers and grasses. Explore the nearby iron-age cross dykes, or go a little further for historic castles and grand houses. The easy-going and friendly Kerridges don't stop at simply restoring old buildings: veteran car enthusiasts will drool over Tim's collection of classics including a magnificent 1930s Lagonda.

sleeps	2.
price	£200–£350.
rooms	1 double; bath & wc.
closed	Never.

booking details

Tim & Lucy Kerridge

tel	01747 811881
fax	01747 811881
e-mail	theoldforge@hotmail.com

map 3   entry 38

Boot & Shoe Cottage
Wycliffe, Durham

Pure *Wind in the Willows*: the waters of the River Tees pass the bottom of your garden – hire a rod and fish for trout for £12 a day. The 300-year-old cottage was once a cobbler's home, hence its name; the Peats found leather lasts during their renovation work. All is simple, fresh and immaculate within. A big open fire built of stone is the focal point of the comfy sitting room, where pale shades and crisp white woodwork blend beautifully with country antiques. The kitchen is compact but perfect; its dining end has a table by the woodburner and French windows opening onto the terrace with roses, barbecue and steps to the river. Sunshine streams through the window of the cream-walled double bedroom with its ancient wooden headboard and cast iron fire; under the rafters is a fun little eyrie for children. For groups of six, the Peats will gladly let you use their own very attractive spare room which is accessible from the cottage; it has coral pink walls, chintzy curtains and lovely brass twin beds. You are two miles from an excellent farm shop: rustle up a picnic and walk the glorious Teesdale Way. *Children must be watched by the river.*

sleeps	4.
price	£290–£395.
rooms	2: 1 double; 1 twin; bath & wc.
closed	Never.

booking details

	Mrs Rachel Peat
tel	01833 627200
fax	01833 627200
e-mail	info@bootandshoecottage.co.uk
web	www.bootandshoecottage.co.uk

Froyz Hall Barn
Halstead, Essex

On one side of the big barn door, deeply rural Essex; on the other, oodles of Mediterranean charm. Blue-stained floorboards, a freestanding wooden kitchen, colour-washed brick, delightful crockery and a loft-like stair. You'll love the feel of it all. The 'welcome pack' sets the tone, convincing you – as if you needed it – that you have made a happy landing: a litre of red wine, home-baked bread, unsalted butter, oat cakes, eggs and fresh fruit, and there are Molton Brown goodies in the bathroom to spoil you further. The large, old granary barn has been furnished with lavish generosity: country *armoires*, large beds, Designers Guild linen, piping hot showers to dive into, luxurious towels to cocoon you. The kitchen is magnificently equipped. French windows give onto the pool which has a gated entrance for safety; horses, Labradors, chickens, goats, hayloft and 1,000 working-farm acres ensure your children will be as profoundly happy as you. There's tennis, and a trampoline, and you may fish on the lake. Judi is a delightful mix of competence and smiliness, and Halstead is enchanting.

sleeps	7-9 + baby.
price	£495-£795.
rooms	3: 1 double with bath & wc; 1 triple; 1 twin; 2 showers & wcs. Sofabed/s in main hall.
closed	Never.

booking details

Mike & Judi Butler

tel	01787 476684
fax	01787 474647
e-mail	judy@supanet.com

 map 4   entry 40

Bury Barn Cottage
Pleshey, Essex

Your converted barn, darkly wooded on the outside, is as spotless and as sparkling inside as can be. Your friendly hosts are a minute away, should you need them – the family has transformed several old farm buildings into a combined home, cottage and bedroom-furniture-making business. (And you could not ask for better made oak beds!). Bury Barn Cottage is single storey and open plan. Step inside: the bathroom is ahead of you, the kitchen and living area are to the right, and the bedroom at the end snuggles behind a book-lined shelving unit – with TV that can be swivelled round for night or morning viewing. Perfect. Furniture is attractive and new, rugs and sofabed blue, curtains coral and turquoise; floors are varnished, walls are white. Your starter pack includes fruit, and the Morrises are happy to provide you with a breakfast hamper or evening meal at extra cost – just ask. Two good pubs serve food and Essex ale in the village; shops are a couple of miles off. This is an attractive, warm, comfortable place for a couple (with child) to stay – splendid walks from the door, and a large garden you are welcome to share.

sleeps	2-4.
price	£200–£350.
rooms	1 twin; sofabed; bath, shower & wc.
closed	Never.

booking details

Mr Richard Morris

tel	01245 237384
fax	01245 237327
e-mail	rmorris@richardmorrisfurniture.com
web	www.burybarncottage.co.uk

Garden Studio

Compton Abdale, Gloucestershire

French windows lead onto a terrace and a simple lawned garden with fruit trees. The view is of the sort that one dreams of when caught in a heat-wave in North Africa: rolling fields and gentle Cotswold hills, unfolding into the unimaginable distance. Come for all-embracing peace, for a deep sense of calm. The serenity comes, too, from Mrs Smail – a reflexologist at a local hospice and a delightful woman, caring and considerate. The house, in the old stable-block, is one-storey and open plan in traditional style, simple yet light, airy and comfortable, rather like a large studio. There are fresh flowers, lots of cushions, stripey rugs, good pictures, plenty of books. It would be easy to use for someone in a wheelchair, though not officially so. You'll need your own transport as shops are a few miles away, though Mrs Smail will do your shopping before you arrive if you ask. The main house and gardens are lovely, as you'd expect in this part of England. *Stable Cottage with log-burner and private garden sleeps 4.*

sleeps	2-3.
price	£110–£240.
rooms	1 double; bath & wc; extra bed in living area.
closed	Never.

booking details

Mrs Louise Smail

tel	01242 890263
fax	01242 890266
e-mail	springhillcottages@yahoo.co.uk

map 3   entry 42

Wayside Cottage
Painswick, Gloucestershire

Painswick has earned the title 'The Queen of the Cotswolds' and a brief visit reveals why. Every building and quaint street of this medieval wool town is 'character filled', every garden overflows with flowers; you have probably seen Painswick in some costume drama on TV. Overlooking the splendid church and its famous yews, Wayside is a typical example of an 18th-century Painswick townhouse, and has been sensitively and imaginatively restored. Historic and modern elements have been seamlessly brought together; all rooms have a feeling of space and light and have old stone fireplaces, really nice furniture and oodles of character. Good paintings and pretty plates hang on walls; an old newspaper that blocked one of the fireplaces, now framed, makes fascinating reading. The beamed sitting room encourages deep sloth and the main bedroom is serenely gorgeous. The attractive, wooden floored kitchen is very well equipped. You get a smiley welcome and home-made apricot flapjacks from your hostess, fresh flowers in every room. All this plus plentiful and unusual shops, lots of pubs and eateries and the oldest bowling green in England.

sleeps	4 + baby.
price	£250–£550.
rooms	3: 1 double; 2 singles; bath & wc.
closed	Occasionally.

booking details

	Mark Ottignon
tel	01452 813589

The Coach House
Bushley, Gloucestershire

A superbly renovated Victorian coach house, whose long, fine roof and spruce exterior reflect the harmony within. A generous hallway leads into a big, light living room with, at one end, easy chairs and open fire (perfect for crumpet-toasting); at the other, antique dresser and dining table. Fling open the French windows in summer to patio and birdsong. The large and airy kitchen has a range-style cooker with a dazzling array of features to tempt the most reluctant cook; luxury underfloor heating runs throughout. Bedrooms are pretty, uncluttered, carpeted in soft grey blue, with divinely comfortable beds; one has strikingly original beams and a view of an ancient spreading walnut tree. Peace reigns. The village is a tranquil haven, and there's a small country garden overlooking glebe land just for you. Not to be missed are the old stones from the church, some with gargoyle-like faces, lining the drive to the vicarage where the Davises live. They are delightful people who are much involved with village life. You are well placed for both the Cheltenham Races and the Malvern Hills.

sleeps	4.
price	£450–£600.
rooms	2: 1 double with bath & wc; 1 double; shower & wc.
closed	Never.

booking details

	Sue Davis
tel	01684 296431
e-mail	sue@cozy-toes.co.uk
web	www.cozy-toes.co.uk

map 3   entry 44

Upper Court & courtyard cottages

Kemerton, Gloucestershire

Terrific for just two people or for the big family reunion. The same seriously comfortable, stylish feel applies to all five properties around the splendidly Georgian Upper Court. And all benefit from the lake (boat available) and 15 acres of grounds and lovely gardens. The Herfords love antiques and their classic good taste, along with a real understanding of what's needed (they've been welcoming guests for 30 years) make for a happy experience. Garden Flat sleeps two in cosy splendour, the Stables five (two in a ground floor half-tester bed), Courtyard Cottage, eight, the Watermill, with its own lakeside garden, 10, and the Coach House up to 11. The sitting/dining room here is huge, with three sofas and two long dining tables: perfect for special get-togethers (catering and maid service can be arranged). Woodburning stoves, 'secret' doors, good bathrooms, well-equipped kitchens; an outdoor pool (June-Sept) surrounded by exotic plants, an all-weather tennis court, croquet, table tennis and the Cotswolds on your doorstep. Perfect for a celebration weekend for up to 36. Quite a place!

sleeps	2; 5; 8; 10; 11.
price	£275–£1,465.
rooms	**GF** 1 double/twin with shower & wc. **S** 1 double, bath, shower & wc; 1 double; 1 single; wc. **CC** 1 double & 2 singles; 1 double; 1 twin; bath & wc; shower & wc. **W** 1 triple, bath & wc; 3 doubles; 1 single; bath & wc; shower & wc. **CH** 1 triple, shower & wc; 2 doubles, bath & wc; 1 double; 1 twin, bath & wc; wc.
closed	Never.

booking details

Bill & Diana Herford

tel	01386 725351
fax	01386 725472
e-mail	diana@uppercourt.co.uk
web	www.uppercourt.co.uk

Waterfall Cottage

Burley, Hampshire

The 1840 cottage is set in gardens planted by a Chelsea gold-medallist; embraced by stream, waterfall and trees, its lawns lead directly to New Forest heathland and forest dotted with ponies and deer... it is quintessentially English, a magical place. John used to paddle in the stream as a boy – his aunt (the gardener) lived here; he and Naomi have put love and energy into making the cottage a beautiful place to stay. It is light and sunny and full of family antiques – a Georgian bookcase here, a portrait of great-grandmama there. Elegance and cottage cosiness combine in restored parquet floors, Farrow & Ball walls, velvet drapes, fresh flowers, Aga and working coal and log fire. Off a big landing are three eiderdowned bedrooms: the master with its own dressing room and tiny, wisteria-clad balcony, the twin with hugely wide floorboards and goatskin rugs, the little single with sloped ceiling and Victorian bed. Pubs, shops, bike-hire and horse-drawn carriages are a mile off; walks are on the spot. And everywhere, the song of birds and stream: it's like stumbling upon a hidden corner of England.

sleeps	5 + baby.
price	£300–£900.
rooms	3: 1 double; 1 twin; 1 single; bath; 2 wcs.
closed	Never.

booking details

Naomi & John King
tel 01722 334337
fax 01722 555547

map 3   entry 46

Kilvert's Cottage
Winforton, Herefordshire

A glorious area, the Wye Valley, and Winforton is one of the hidden pleasures of this delightful neck of the Welsh Borders woods. Kilvert's Cottage has something special about it, too; it may look as if it's been standing in the terraced gardens of Winforton Court since Shakespeare was a boy, but it was built in 1984. (To give the cottage some historical ballast, the Gothic front door was rescued from the village school where curate-diarist Francis Kilvert once taught.) Half-timbered, long and handsome, with a large and lovely garden, the place oozes character; it is roomy, light and as clean as a new pin, yet without a whiff of cold carbolic – a comfortable house with a friendly spirit. A welcome hamper and flowers; a good-sized dining room; bedrooms light and airy; a vast view from the first-floor sitting room across garden and fields to the Black Mountains beyond. Young bookworms will be enchanted by the story books and miniature armchairs for children, while adults may use Winforton Court's library... or plunder the world-famous second-hand bookshops of nearby Hay-on-Wye. *Laundry room at Winforton Court. Fishing can be arranged.*

sleeps	4 + baby.
price	£220–£390.
rooms	2: 1 double; 1 twin; bath, shower & wc.
closed	Never.

booking details

	Jackie Kingdon
tel	01544 328498
fax	01544 328498

The Woolhouse Barn

Hunton, Kent

Such a clever conversion of a more than 350-year-old Grade II listed barn. Every pain has been taken and the result is cosily, comfortably characterful. If you love ancient oak beams, slopey ceilings, unusual angles and beautifully co-ordinated fabrics, furniture and paintwork you'll find it hard to tear yourself away. The unusual layout makes the most logical use of space – and there's something about a house with two stairs. The main bedroom with its shower room is on the ground floor, the other two bedrooms and bathroom immediately above; the fitted, everything-you-need kitchen/dining room and delightfully cosy two-sofa sitting room are also on the first floor, up the second stair. Halogen lights illuminate the beamed ceilings; rugs, prints, plates, books and ornaments make it homely. And then there's outside… a pretty private garden area where you can eat and oversee the activities of the alpacas; conservation area countryside; and masses to see and do all around, with stately homes and wonderful gardens and family activities. The owners are next door if needed and couldn't be more helpful.

sleeps	4-5.
price	£250-£425.
rooms	3: 1 double with shower & wc; 1 twin; 1 single; bath & wc.
closed	Christmas & New Year.

booking details

Gavin & Anne Wetton

tel	01622 820778
fax	01622 820645
e-mail	anne@wetton.info.co.uk
web	www.wetton.info.co.uk

 map 4   entry 48

Mill Hill Cottage
Little Steeping, Lincolnshire

In a patchwork landscape of fields sits a perfect example of the 'mud and stud' building unique to Lincolnshire: clay, straw and water applied 'wattle and daub' style to a timber frame, topped off with a canopy of exquisitely maintained thatch. The newly-restored farmworker's cottage is in tip-top condition, the brick floor gleaming, the limewashed walls blemish-free, the vast cast iron range blacked to perfection. Enter via a small hallway, with dining room and kitchen/pantry to right, bathroom and sitting room, with sofa, sofabed and open coal fire, to left. Bedrooms sit snugly under the eaves; the double is reached via a stairway from the dining room, the twin up an excitingly steep, half-twist ladder stair – unsuitable for the infirm or very young. The rooms are furnished in keeping with the status of the building: painted ladder-back chairs, cream wrought-iron bedstead, two armchairs in blue check. Simple and beautiful. Visit the shops of market towns Spilsby and Horncastle, eat well in the village pub, walk the Viking Way... or bask in the garden of this Vivat Trust gem in the heart of Lord Alfred Tennyson country.

sleeps	4-5 + 1 baby.
price	£540–£695.
rooms	2: 1 double; 1 twin; sofabed; bath & wc.
closed	Never.

booking details

Vivat Trust

tel	0845 090 0194
fax	0845 090 0174
e-mail	enquiries@vivat.org.uk
web	www.vivat.org.uk

Dovecote

Cley next the Sea, Norfolk

Among the wild salt marshes of north Norfolk, where land and sea appear to mingle with the towering sky, Dovecote seems to have its feet in the water. The wind whistles gently across the reeds from the sea only hundreds of yards away and Blakeney, with its wild sea birds, is no distance. It is a magical, beautiful and unusual place. The Mill – once windmill, now hotel – is one of the great landmarks of this coast and a convivial place to have a drink or meal; Jeremy does wonders with local ingredients and he or his staff are always on hand. The Dovecote is one of The Mill's outbuildings, built of that attractive Norfolk combination of flint, brick and tile. It is a modest conversion, nothing chic, just sensible and homely: striped red and white curtains, pine tongue-and-groove panelling, pine furniture, pine kitchen units and practical lino floor. There's a staircase to the mezzanine and the double bedroom and another charming little room downstairs. The Mill has a big garden right by the little river, surrounded by reeds and peace. The sunsets from here are unforgettably lovely. *You can also rent the Longhouse and the Boathouse, both a little smaller.*

sleeps	4.
price	£290–£430.
rooms	2: 1 double; 1 twin; bath & wc.
closed	Never.

booking details

	Jeremy Bolam
tel	01263 740209
fax	01263 740209

map 8   entry 50

Barn Cottage

Toft Monks, Norfolk

Flemish weavers washed their flax in the moat surrounding the exceptionally pretty Queen Anne mansion, then dried it in the next-door barn. This is the larger of two newly restored cottages (see also Meadow Cottage) and forms part of the courtyard of the Grade II*-listed house. Furnishings are elegant and traditional. The kitchen is huge – always a joy – with old pine dresser, table and chairs, heaps of work space and absolutely everything you need. Pale, creamy bedrooms – two big, two smaller – look onto peaceful soft Suffolk farmland; the twins on the ground floor share a spacious bathroom; the doubles upstairs have their own bathrooms, and the main bedroom has a super king-size bed. The woodburning stove enhances the sitting room although the whole place is centrally heated. Both cottages have private gardens with barbecues and furniture. Head down to the River Waveney for the Norfolk Broads or give your hosts advance notice if you'd like a mooring or to try your hand at coarse-fishing. They'll happily let you use their tennis court, too. *Also entry 52.*

sleeps	8.
price	£525-£775.
rooms	4: 2 doubles with bath & wc; 2 twins; bath & wc.
closed	Occasionally.

booking details

Richard & Teena Freeland

tel	01502 677380
fax	01502 677362
e-mail	richardfreeland@btconnect.com
web	www.freelandenterprises.co.uk

Meadow Cottage
Toft Monks, Norfolk

Here is a heavenly hideaway in the tranquil grounds of The Elms, a splendid red brick Queen Anne mansion. Smaller than neighbouring Barn Cottage (see entry 51), it is every bit as beautifully restored, spotlessly clean and well-equipped with all you need including dishwasher. The living/dining/kitchen rooms are combined in a single space, furnished with a mix of stylish but traditional modern furniture and old farmhouse pine. The outlook is green and pleasant. The double rooms are simple and attractive, and there's a cosy attic feel to the twin room; traditional Suffolk flooring bricks with kilim and seagrass in the living area; carpeted main bedroom. Both cottages have private gardens with barbecue and sitting out areas. Numerous woodland walks lead down to the River Waveney (one and a half miles) in this beautiful, unspoiled area. The Norfolk Broads are reachable by river and mooring can be arranged via the owners; tennis and course fishing too. You are four miles to the nearest shops; a visit to the old market towns of Beccles and Bungay is a must. *Also entry 51.*

sleeps	6.
price	£450–£575
rooms	3: 1 double with shower & wc; 1 double; 1 twin; bath & wc.
closed	Occasionally.

booking details

Richard & Teena Freeland

tel	01502 677380
fax	01502 677362
e-mail	richardfreeland@btconnect.com
web	www.freelandenterprises.co.uk

map 8   entry 52

The Coastguard Lodge

Belford, Northumberland

Drive through the security gate, down the private lane, pull up at the cottage and abandon the car: everything is here for a restorative break. You stay in a magnificent Victorian brick-built building that used to house the vehicle which fired rocket lines to troubled ships; down the lane and over the dunes is what feels like your very own beach (being Northumberland, this means three miles of perfect white, clean, deserted sand). In the converted lodge are large rooms, wooden floors and good lighting. Bedrooms are pretty with patchwork quilts and great views and the cheerful sitting room has yellow walls, pale wood chairs, a checked sofa and an attractive electric fire. To the front is your own walled, sunny garden; in the yard, a laundry (shared with other cottages). There is excellent walking straight from the house, boat trips to the Farne Isles to see the puffins, outings to Bamburgh and Holy Island castles, and local bike hire. The beach may beckon most strongly. At the end of the day, another treat… an 'honesty' freezer packed to the brim with good home-cooked dishes. *Other cottages at Outchester Farm.*

sleeps	5.
price	£241–£557.
rooms	3: 1 double; 1 twin; 1 single; 2 baths & wcs.
closed	Never.

booking details

John Sutherland

tel	01668 213336
fax	01668 219385
e-mail	enquiry@rosscottages.co.uk
web	www.rosscottages.co.uk

Firwood Bungalow

Nr Middleton Hall, Northumberland

Aga enthusiasts will be thrilled with their very own oil-fired friend in the lino-floored, rag-rugged farmhouse kitchen. Here is a one-storey, higgledy-piggledy Victorian house in a hamlet at the foot of the Cheviots in the Northumberland National Park. Trot from the kitchen to the courtyard (with barbecue), round to the front door and into the hall (with original mosaic floor): children enjoy the circuit. Everything is big: the bedrooms, the utility room for drying clothes and wellies, the dining and sitting rooms with open fireplaces – coal and logs provided. Touches of elegance too as Sylvia collects antiques. Exhaust the children to an early bed, then relax over a candlelit dinner at the gleaming table. This is wonderful place for large groups – up to 12 can be bedded – with one and a half acres of landscaped gardens (64 species of bird recorded in one week) and super views. Wooler is close with good shops, pubs and bikes to hire. Superb walking, riding and wildlife, an easy drive to all those fabulous beaches, and the Farne Isles for seals. *Annexed cottage with conservatory and private garden sleeps 6.*

sleeps	10-12 + baby.
price	£200-£750.
rooms	3: 2 doubles, 1 with extra double, 1 with extra single; 1 twin with extra single; sofabed; bath & wc; shower & wc. Also two extra beds to put up wherever.
closed	Never.

booking details

	Mr & Mrs Charles Armstrong
tel	01665 579443
fax	01665 579407
e-mail	N.Charlton1@plus.net
web	www.northcharlton.com

map 10   entry 54

Catherine's Barn

Alnmouth, Northumberland

Naturalists will love the rare animals and birds, walkers will stride from Cheviots to coast, sportsmen will fish and shoot. Sybarites will kick their shoes off, put the stereo on and enjoy the soft carpets and cosiness of this spanking new conversion. Along one side of the 1715 farmhouse courtyard is your cottage, one of three; downstairs are bedrooms with good beds and linen, doors with pine latches, loads of beams and sparkling bath/shower room. Upstairs to a huge open-plan, halogen-lit sitting room, more beams, good sofas, cream walls and long views across hills to sea through great dormer windows. An L-shaped modern kitchen is bursting with equipment and has a good-sized table for lounging around. White sandy beaches are a hop away, there is a wave of castles, pele towers and Roman remains to please history buffs, and lively Newcastle is a short drive with its shopping, theatre, clubs and culture – great for townies and teenagers. Make the most of your friendly hosts; Brian and Dorothy are busy farming 390 acres but always have time for their guests and know every inch of this gorgeous county.

sleeps	4.
price	£200–£450.
rooms	1 double; 1 double/twin; bath, shower & wc.
closed	Never.

booking details

Brian & Dorothy Jackson

tel	01665 830427
fax	01665 830063
e-mail	dorothy@biltonbarns.co.uk
web	www.biltonbarns.co.uk

Out of Bounds

Foxton, Northumberland

Smack on the Northumbrian coast just north of Alnmouth, a cottage in a matchless position. The garden slopes right down to the beach (lively toddlers beware) and the sea comes in to the bedrooms: you could not find a sandier, saltier spot for a holiday house. Step inside and you'll be equally delighted with your fresh, airy, comfortable home-from-home: good new pine, white linen sofas, checked fabrics, rattan and rugs. Get the logs going in the sitting room, curl up on the padded seat by the window – the views are stunning up and down Foxton Bay. Or retreat with a glass of wine to the cosy bedrooms – more views! You can take your meals in the windproof suntrap of an enclosed patio, or eat *al fresco* on the sundeck outside. Being Northumberland, there's no knowing just how fresco things may get along this bracing coast, so don't forget to slip the woollens into the suitcase along with the swimming gear, and close the large curtains in the sitting room at night. Walks all around, and Alnmouth golf course just round the corner. Perfect for outward bounders.

sleeps	6 + 1 child.
price	£495–£895.
rooms	3: 1 double with extra single; 2 twins; bath & wc; 2 showers & wcs.
closed	Christmas week.

booking details

	Hazel Tate
tel	07973 310055
e–mail	golftate@aol.com

map 10 entry 56

High Buston Hall

High Buston, Northumberland

Therese of High Buston Hall has huge energy and flair; husband Ian backs her to the hilt. They are a delightful couple and have renovated the old servants' quarters – your little cottage – in the best possible way. Everything is as neat as ninepence and as clean as a whistle – yet bursting with character too. The kitchen is a craftsman's dream, and you want for nothing (breadmaker, microwave, dishwasher). Seagrass over terracotta tiles and elegant country furnishings give a cosy feel; any Northumbrian nip in the air is dispelled by the woodburning stove downstairs and the soft-as-goosedown pillows up. Beds are antique with good mattresses, the shower's fabulous and you'd pay good money to see the view from the loo: it sweeps over farmland and estuary to the sea. You have your own secluded patio, and Therese and Ian are also very happy for you to roam the Hall's recently terraced and replanted gardens. Away beyond the bounds of Buston this is castle country: Warkworth, Alnwick and Dunstanburgh are all within bow-shot, while along the coast the cleanest and emptiest beaches in England beckon.

sleeps	4.
price	£395–£595.
rooms	2: 1 double with bath & wc; 1 twin with shower & wc.
closed	Never.

booking details

Ian & Therese Atherton

tel	01665 830606
fax	01665 830707
e-mail	enquiries@highbuston.com
web	www.members.aol.com/highbuston

Quarry House

Longhorsley, Northumberland

Is it a bird? Is it a plane? No, it's Alun – zooming around on his electric golf caddy making sure all is serene. And, of course, it is. The single-storey sandstone Quarry House is the recently-built (12 years ago) second farmhouse to Beacon Hill Farm – in its own grounds yet a stroll from swimming pool, jacuzzi and gym, shared with other guests. Everything you could possibly need or want is here from an endless variety of sporting things to do – walking, riding, fishing – to the huge farmhouse kitchen with two fridges and loads of gadgets. The drawing room is enormous, with open fire, antiques and comfy chairs, long views over miles of Northumberland and doors that open into your garden, perfect for *al fresco* suppers. Large light rooms with vast windows, good beds, pristine bathrooms with terrific showers, lovely paintings, books galore. You have 360 acres at the door: lakes, grassland dotted with ponies and mature beech woods teeming with red squirrels. The views are glorious.

sleeps	6 + baby.
price	£440–£1,200
rooms	3: 1 double; 2 twins; bath & wc; shower & wc.
closed	Never.

booking details

Alun Moore

tel	01670 780900
fax	01670 780901
e-mail	alun@beaconhill.co.uk
web	www.beaconhill.co.uk

 map 10   entry 58

The Old Byre
Slaley, Northumberland

Bring all the family – and Granny, too: there's plenty of room. This is rural heaven for large groups and children will adore it. You stay in the old milking byre which is one of a collection of outbuildings around the small, typically Northumbrian working farm. The large square entrance hall has vinyl flooring, so no need to worry about mud, and leads to a big kitchen/dining room with all the mod cons and a wooden table big enough for the whole brood. After the rigours of family catering, collapse into comfy seats in the cream-painted, carpeted sitting room end where the woodburner glows. Downstairs is a large twin with extra bed and walk-in shower (perfect for those who cannot manage stairs). The furniture and decoration is not posh, but clean and bright and the bathrooms sparkle. Great views from all the windows – you won't miss the pig, it's enormous! – and you can see the hills from all the big beamed bedrooms. If the weather's not kind, there is a games room and Barn Skittle Alley (with barbecue); further on, a laundry room for wet clothes. Outside, a pretty walled garden, a summer house, great walking, good pubs, shops, fishing, riding and cycling.

sleeps	9 + baby.
price	£350-£700.
rooms	4: 1 double with bath & wc; 1 twin (plus single trundle bed) with bath & wc; 1 triple (as double and single or 3 singles); 1 single; bath & wc.
closed	Never.

booking details

	Elizabeth Courage
tel	01434 673259
fax	01434 673259
e-mail	info@ryehillfarm.co.uk
web	www.ryehillfarm.co.uk

Carter's Cottage & Orchard Cottage
Northmoor, Oxfordshire

These two little cottages would be perfect for two families staying together; they are identical, separated only by a fence in the garden and thus open to each other. They have been created from an 18th-century open-fronted cart shed on a 400-acre farm in an Environmentally Sensitive Area. The countryside is, of course, glorious: river meadows, canal boats idling along the Thames – which runs through the farmland. Perfect for less-than-energetic cyclists, especially along the towpath. Back in the cottages: a good-sized kitchen with flagstones and all you need, open to the rest of the house. The furniture is practical and simple, in keeping with the farmhouse style. It is easy and relaxed, plain and attractive, nothing stuffy or stylish. Open-brick fireplace, pine chests, plain walls and carpets, fresh flowers. Mary Anne is down-to-earth and immensely helpful, a busy farmer's wife but available to help. The family has farmed here for three generations and they are willing to show you the farm and the animals. Great for children – and safe.

sleeps	4.
price	£240–£400.
rooms	2: 1 double; 1 twin; bath & wc; shower & wc.
closed	Never.

booking details

Mary Anne & Robert Florey

tel	01865 300207
fax	01865 300559
e-mail	PJ.Florey@farmline.com
web	www.oxtowns.co.uk/rectoryfarm

map 3   entry 60

Glebe Cottage
Westwell, Oxfordshire

An 18th-century stone house and its cottage wing sit behind a Norman church in a perfect Cotswold hamlet. "England at its most idyllic," said our inspector. Westwell is an ancient place and the setting is a dream; there was a Roman villa here once, beside the spring that feeds the village pond. Your cottage is next to the main house but you are as private as can be, with your own west-facing terrace and grassy, apple-tree garden gated from fields; house-martins swoop, pigeons coo. Inside all is light, bright and fresh: simple furniture, white walls, wooden and coir floors, a small kitchen thoughtfully equipped. The twin bedroom feels cottagey with its white-painted rafters and a little balcony overlooking stables and countryside; the double has a French feel (the Dunipaces have strong French connections) with soft yellow-patterned walls and gorgeous white bedcover. Clare and Robin are very friendly and welcome you with a bottle of a favourite French wine. Children can join one of the art and craft workshops the Dunipaces organise in the holidays, play in the secret tree 'fort' or ride a pony – just ask. Westwell is a gem.

sleeps	2-6.
price	£250-£550.
rooms	1 double; 1 twin/double; bath; wc; sofabed also available.
closed	Never.

booking details

Clare & Robin Dunipace

tel	01993 822171
fax	01993 824125
e-mail	clare.dunipace@amserve.net
web	www.oxford-cotswold-holidays.com

Arley Cottage
Hook Norton, Oxfordshire

This tiny fairy-tale cottage gives its guests a big welcome. Perhaps there is a touch of magic about the small decanter of sherry, eggs, bread, coffee and tea which greet them; the beaming gnome by the front door may have the answer. Pictures of the countryside and a profusion of ornaments – china owls, rose petals in a crystal basket, sea shells in the bathroom, a family of mice in lacy dresses on the pine shelves of the kitchen – all find their place in this spotless nest. There's a gateleg table for two, embroidered arm covers on the sofa and chairs and a stone fireplace with attendant log basket. Royal Doulton china, flowery Egyptian cotton on the duvet, bird and flower prints – and gorgeous wooded valley views. Mrs Merc next door, a hunting lady, keeps an eye on things from her loose box. Beyond the staddle stones, pretty garden and pedigree grey-faced Dartmoors, an old railway line leads into a nature reserve and the glowing ironstone walls of this country bordering the Cotswolds. A Rural Fair in the village in July, and annual folk and beer festivals too.

sleeps	2.
price	£210–£310.
rooms	1 double; bath & wc.
closed	Never.

booking details

	Nicola McHugh
tel	01608 737217
e-mail	shaunmchugh@btinternet.com

map 3   entry 62

Mill Stream Cottage

Clun, Shropshire

Wake to the music of birdsong and river – all you'll hear in your nest by the River Unk. Birches Mill was built with its cottage in 1640, and corn was ground here right up until the Second World War. Gill and Andrew – artists, home cooks, growers of fine organic produce – run a B&B next door: share a meal at their table. You can buy their preserves too. This is a beautiful conversion, where kitchen, living and dining areas blend into one: painted terracotta floorboards, beautiful beams, red squishy sofa, cast-iron woodburner, windows made of local timber to the original design. The kitchen is small, special: handmade wooden units with old brass fittings are painted duck-egg-blue, topped with quarry tiles; there are plenty of utensils and a great new electric oven. Climb the coir-carpeted stair to your skylit bedroom with views, where pine bed and dressing table have a well-loved patina; step out of the chunky front door (handmade, naturally) into picture-perfect, deepest Shropshire. Footpaths lead to Offa's Dyke, one mile away; forts, farmers' markets and castles wait to be explored. *Miller's House, with wildflower garden, sleeps four.*

sleeps	2.
price	£210–£350.
rooms	1 double with bath & wc.
closed	Never.

booking details

Gill Della Casa & Andrew Farmer

tel	01588 640409
fax	01588 640409
web	www.virtual-shropshire.co.uk/ millstreamcottage

Dick Turpin's Cottage
Clun, Shropshire

An extravaganza, an entertainment created with a twinkle in the eye. Come to have your spirits lifted. Our inspector went into a mild form of ecstasy, overwhelmed by the imaginative, luxurious eccentricity of it all. There is – why not? – a clock from a Russian submarine in the bathroom, with a pig diving into the village pond above the bath. And an array of bathrobes, umbrellas, kitchen equipment, and CD speakers set into ceilings; press a button on the wall of the sitting room and the sound floods in. The space is vast and generous: a long, light hall and huge sitting/dining room with terrific fireplace (all the logs you need) and sculpture above it. The fabrics on the chairs and great sofa are colourful and expensive, the views are deep and glorious. The kitchen is pine-floored and of polished granite. The 'welcome' pack is as large as a Harrods' hamper. The bedroom has heavily patterned fabric wallpaper, like a Turkish carpet; the shower is gargantuan. Behind the cottage are 200 acres of wilderness and wildlife, with a log path built into the hillside to make your walk flawless. Roger has thought of everything.

sleeps	2.
price	£400–£555.
rooms	1 twin/double; bath & wc.
closed	Never.

booking details

	Roger Wren
tel	01588 640327
fax	01588 640881
e-mail	cockford.hall@virgin.net
web	www.dickturpincottage.com

map 6   entry 64

The Temple
Badger, Shropshire

The approach – through a tree-lined carriageway, woods, huge gates – is an adventure in itself. "One of the most breathtaking places I've ever seen," said our inspector. Can there be a more idyllic hideaway for two? You are as secluded as can be and the 1783 folly – built to complement Badger Hall – is as delightful inside as out. There are Persian rugs on wooden floors, deep Regency-striped sofas piled high with cushions, fine prints and painted furniture inspired by architect James Wyatt's original designs, fresh flowers... more comfort and style than you could have dared hope for. Breakfast or lunch on a colonnaded balcony overlooking the Dingle, a 40-acre fantasy created by a pupil of Capability Brown; hidden within its sandstone chasms and wooden ravines are an icehouse, a rotunda, pools and tunnels and wildlife. The kitchen has beech worktops, matt red units and terracotta floor, the bedroom a French double bed with pale yellow striped silk headboards and antique washstand; the walk-in shower has a head like a dinner plate and works like a monsoon. A magical place.

sleeps	2.
price	£495–£620
rooms	1 double with shower & wc.
closed	Never.

booking details

	Vivat Trust
tel	0845 090 0194
fax	0845 090 0174
e-mail	enquiries@vivat.org.uk
web	www.vivat.org.uk

The Barn

Betchcott, Shropshire

If there's a quintessential English medieval barn, this is it. Its restoration has been dictated by the great number of ancient beams – it can feel as if you're in the middle of a giant pile of Spillikins! Homely comfort in the living room where there's plenty of space for eating, relaxing and playing games. The kitchen is very well equipped, and the cutlery and crockery are of good quality; the washing machine is in a building across the courtyard. More comfort in the bedrooms; the carpeted double on the ground floor has its own bath and shower, and a lovely view. The twin rooms under the sloping roof line are equally pleasing; one is right opposite the upstairs bathroom while the other is perhaps more suitable for children, who can trot down one staircase and up another to reach the bathroom. An enclosed terrace runs the length of the building and has fabulous views; in unending folds of hills, this is a paradise for walkers. The feel thoughout the barn is happily unfussy, welcoming and cheerful, and the friendly owners live next door. *Two other cottages also available.*

sleeps	6.
price	£280-£500.
rooms	3: 1 double with bath, shower & wc; 2 twins; bath & wc.
closed	Occasionally.

booking details

	Mrs Anne Carter
tel	01694 751232
fax	01694 751232
e-mail	batchcote@aol.com
web	www.virtual-shropshire.co.uk/middlefarm

 map 6   entry 66

Garden Cottage
Westbury, Shropshire

The BBC filmed *Martin Chuzzlewit* here, which tells you a lot about the 'wow' factor of Whitton Hall: an early 18th-century country pile set in glorious, rolling countryside where any self-respecting child would give his or her milk teeth to grow up. The warm brick of Garden Cottage is reflected in the pretty little lake beside the Hall – it's an entirely unpretentious place with a lived-in feel. Come with a couple of chums or a clutch of kids – for a short break or longer – without worrying about someone knocking over a Ming vase or spoiling a priceless piece of Chippendale with their muddy wellies. Nothing fragile or too precious here: a beamy sitting room has solid Edwardian furniture with a cheery open fire and a clubby feel. The lino-floored kitchen is simple; bedrooms a hot-potch of furniture. Stroll through the woods, laze by the lake, borrow a bike from the friendly Hallidays or sit with your dogs and children in the the sunny, walled garden or by the pool. The more energetic can strike out with a map and a sandwich into the glorious hill country all around.

sleeps	4.
price	£265–£300.
rooms	2: 1 double; 1 twin; bath & wc.
closed	Christmas & New Year.

booking details

	Christopher & Gill Halliday
tel	01743 884270
fax	01743 884158
e-mail	whittonhall@farmersweekly.net

The Summerhouse

Eyton-on-Severn, Shropshire

Sir Francis Newport, Comptroller of the Royal Household during Charles II's reign, used to live on this estate and the Summerhouse is 'all' that remains today. It's a rare, octagonal Jacobean banqueting tower with a balustraded roof terrace – perfect for stargazing from! – that gives onto Eyton race course and the sweeping Shropshire countryside. Such elevated banqueting towers were built a fair way from the big house; dinner guests would repair to them for spiced wine, sweetmeats and views. Today you have wine in the fridge, an open fire in the bed/sitting room, a regally canopied four-poster bed, opulent drapes at the window, and arcaded French windows onto the garden. Once you've roused yourself from your dream state, the Long Mynd and the Wrekin offer wild and stupendous walking – and you can put another foot in the past as you explore the remains of the Roman city in Wroxeter. Shrewsbury's shops are 20 minutes away. There could scarcely be a more perfect, fairy-tale intimate retreat for two... but one word of caution: the uneven spiral stairs mean this cannot be the perfect retreat for the infirm.

sleeps	2 + baby.
price	£495-£620.
rooms	1 double; shower & wc.
closed	Never.

booking details

Vivat Trust

tel	0845 090 0194
fax	0845 090 0174
e-mail	enquiries@vivat.org.uk
web	www.vivat.org.uk

 map 6   entry 68

Farm Cottage

Nr Selworthy, Somerset

The organic ethos is strong here. The Webbers care passionately about the environment and animal welfare on their award-winning, 500-acre Exmoor farm, where they tend Aberdeen Angus cattle, rare-breed pigs and sheep. You will be greeted by a small army of ducks on arrival – and a hamper of farm produce on the kitchen table. Penny has brilliantly restored this 1850s worker's cottage: took back the walls to bare brick – exposing a fine fireplace in the sitting room. She even found time to replant the garden. The cottage has an airy feel and is cool and fresh in summer, warm and cosy in winter. Stripped doors, comfy sofas, stylish throughout in buttermilk yellow. It sits in a steeply terraced, fenced garden, where peacocks wander, hewn from the hillside at the head of a beautiful, seemingly remote, tree-lined valley; the only noise you hear is the odd tractor (or peacock). At the Webbers' organic shop you can buy almost everything you need from day to day, and they have mapped out walks and bridle paths over the moor, great for spotting wildlife and views. It's a superb place for riding too – bring your horse. *Farmhouse Wing Cottage and B&B also available at the farmhouse.*

sleeps	2-6.
price	£350-£650.
rooms	3: 2 doubles; 1 room with bunks; bath & wc; shower & wc.
closed	Never.

booking details

	Penny & Roger Webber
tel	01643 705244
fax	01643 705244
e-mail	info@hindonfarm.co.uk
web	www.hindonfarm.co.uk

The Old Priory

Dunster, Somerset

The great carpet invasion stopped short of this house, arrested by the lovely smell of polish on the ocean of wooden floors. This is a place of massive age and honesty. You enter your wing through a vast oak door: the sitting room has stone-mullioned windows, beams, wooden floors and bread oven. The sofa and easy chairs are set against rich dark velvet curtains, there is an open woodburner in the huge hearth, and the room is stuffed with fine old things — drawings, furniture, objects and paintings. All comfortably lived-in; an older era works its magic on you. The dining room is in the kitchen — an oak refectory table and painted cupboard, wicker armchairs, space galore, no dishwasher. The bedrooms, in the same vein, have rugs on wooden floors and views over the big churchyard. The wonderful atmosphere is everywhere, dark and romantic, not gloomy. You may use the walled garden and the rose garden, shared easily with Jane. She is a character, direct and amusing. The setting is simply delightful — next to a magnificent church, with Dunster Castle towering on the hill.

sleeps	4.
price	£175–£600.
rooms	2: 1 double; 1 twin with extra single; bath & wc; wc.
closed	Christmas.

booking details

Jane Forshaw
tel   01643 821540

Enby's Yard

Wambrook, Somerset

A touch of New England on the edge of the Somerset Levels – it's a happy marriage in this barn conversion with mystical views. Local stone, red brick and the original roof tiles were used in its reconstruction; inside, big roof timbers, white plastered walls, a spiral duck-egg-blue staircase, seagrass and terracotta tiles. The main bedroom, simple and serene, has a whitewashed wooden bed, elegant Victorian sofa, lots of light and a wonderful view. More wood in the second bedroom with blue and white gingham curtains and courtyard views – sweet and cosy. The bathroom has white bath, creamy wooden floor and yellow panelling half way up the wall; the kitchen is simple, spotlit, pretty. The garden is bathed in evening and morning sun, and birdsong – and there's a big, rustic table for dining *al fresco*. You'll find a farm shop in Wambrook that stocks organic food, speciality bread and local game – a must for home-cooked evening meals; if you prefer to eat out, it's a 10-minute walk through woods to a good pub in a perfect village. A very special holiday home, also available for shorter breaks, and Lyme Regis only 12 miles away.

sleeps	5 + baby.
price	£200-£400.
rooms	2: 1 double; 1 family room; bath & wc; wc.
closed	Occasionally.

booking details

Patricia & Peter Barbor

tel	01460 61887
e-mail	p.barbor@btopenworld.com

The Old Stables

Castle Cary, Somerset

This is a brand new conversion of the listed old stables, as meticulously executed by the Peppins as the barn. The windows remain small in keeping with 17th-century origins – they are beautifully crafted in dark stained oak with hamstone ledges. The tiled floor is heated throughout. Enter through a glass door into the hall and open plan kitchen and living area... you have a small, superbly equipped kitchen, a wooden dining table, dark blue sofa and armchairs, fine antique corner cupboard, thick tapestry curtains, white walls, chunky beams. The main bedroom is downstairs, simple and cosy with dark-ash four-poster, and bathroom next door. Big upstairs rooms have sloping roofs and red velvet-curtained dormer windows, one with lovely old church boards for its ledge; a gleaming shower lies between. There's a garden all to yourselves – wonderfully private – with newly planted grass, a tree and wooden furniture on the patio. The market town of Castle Cary is down the road, Bath, Longleat and Wells not much further. Lush countryside, delightful hosts, ancient peace... all that's missing are the roses round the door (but, we are assured by Anthea, not for long!). *Also entry 73.*

sleeps	6 + baby.
price	£400–£675.
rooms	3: 1 double; 2 twins; bath & wc; shower & wc.
closed	Never.

booking details

	Anthea Peppin
tel	01963 351288
fax	01963 351288
e-mail	sawdayenq@medievalbarn.co.uk
web	www.medievalbarn.co.uk

map 2   entry 72

The Ancient Barn

Castle Cary, Somerset

Ancient and modern sit in harmony under the dark red roof of this listed medieval cruck barn. It is next to a working farm, its character simple, practical, pleasing. Fresh white lime-plastered walls, exposed beams and a heated flagstone floor – an up-to-date version of the ancient Roman form of heating – set the tone; deep, comfy chairs in sea-green, oriental rugs, a simple pine dresser dotted with country crockery add colour. The kitchen opens into this charming room and is beautifully equipped. The double bedroom is downstairs, cosy with king-sized brass bed and white Indian cover, beige linen curtains at new wooden windows, a shelf of books. The white bathroom has been embellished with hand-painted animals and birds. Upstairs, a more sparsely furnished room with a low cross beam coming between the two beds: perfect for the agile! Patio doors lead from the living room onto a little paved area facing south-west and a quiet road; table and chairs and barbecue too. The Peppins have created a beautiful holiday home and it's very child-friendly, with highchair, plastic cutlery and cot... and the thrill of tractors and cows on the spot. *Also entry 72.*

sleeps	4.
price	£225–£450.
rooms	2: 1 twin; 1 double; bath & wc.
closed	Never.

booking details

	Anthea Peppin
tel	01963 351288
fax	01963 351288
e-mail	sawdayenq@medievalbarn.co.uk
web	www.medievalbarn.co.uk

The Lamb at Pennard Hill Farm

East Pennard, Somerset

The Lamb is a cottage for two, the other 'half' of the Golden Fleece. Much as we shy away from using this sort of language, there is no getting away from it: this is the archetypal "romantic hideaway". Phoebe has transformed her latest interior with typical enthusiasm and talent; it is superb, luxurious, imaginative. There's a large bedroom/dressing room with windows looking north and south – and, as you are 600 feet up on a ridge, the views are over the Somerset Levels and to Glastonbury Tor. All around are acres and acres of perfect farmland, for Phoebe has 100 acres of her own, with Beaulieu sheep, and her neighbour farms organically. Downstairs there is one great open space with everything in it, including a log fire. It is charming, spotlessly clean and sybaritically comfortable – duck and goosedown, original flagstones, heavy, interlined black and white gingham curtains. The black and white theme is everywhere, with metallic touches – restrained and contemporary. What is more, you can use that astonishing indoor pool in the Victorian barn round the corner. What else to say? *Also entry 75.*

sleeps	2.
price	£200 nightly. Please phone for prices of longer stays.
rooms	1 double with bath & wc.
closed	Never.

booking details

Ms Phoebe Judah

tel	01749 890221
fax	01749 890665
e-mail	phebejudah@aol.com
web	www.pennardhillfarm.co.uk

map 2   entry 74

The Fleece at Pennard Hill Farm
East Pennard, Somerset

The cottage overlooks "Tuscan Somerset" – indescribably lovely. Thus wrote visitors, and they were right. Phoebe has a very personal way with décor. She is bold, even adventurous, with colours and with mixing of furniture. With her, nothing is impossible, anything can work – and not just work, but triumph. And Phoebe finds luxury irresistible. So here, 600 feet up, perched on the edge of a ridge with views to Glastonbury Tor and the Somerset Levels, she has transformed a Victorian cottage of stone and brick into something fabulous. The ground floor is an airy, vast space with a huge kitchen and double Aga and everything you could possibly want, from dishwasher on. There is a sunroom and a large drawing room with a handsome open fire. Bedrooms are outrageously comfortable; the bathroom black, white and chrome. You have your own garden leading to fields. Not a sound from traffic – a haven for children, unless they crave noise. And just a step away: a Victorian barn with a vast, beautiful, warm and hazy room that holds – wait for it – a heated pool. A delectable place to stay, worth every penny. *Also entry 74.*

sleeps	7.
price	£450 nightly, with full occupancy. Please phone for prices of longer stays and/or fewer people.
rooms	4: 2 doubles; 1 twin; 1 single; 2 baths & wcs; wc.
closed	Never.

booking details

	Ms Phoebe Judah
tel	01749 890221
fax	01749 890665
e-mail	phebejudah@aol.com
web	www.pennardhillfarm.co.uk

The Turrets
Caverswall, Staffordshire

It's quite old really – 1270 for the stone castle. The rest, rebuilt in 1615, was defortified by Cromwell and then occupied more peaceably – one hopes – by Benedictine nuns. The Wedgwood family lived there in the 1800s, so it has had a distinguished career. It is still massively impressive in many ways, a Jacobean house within a splendid square moat. The two apartments in the turrets are simpler, very much self-catering places rather than extensions of the great house. They are octagonal, small and modestly decorated and an absence of cosy clutter makes for more space. Take some flowers, books and newspapers and a bottle of wine to accompany an instant meal on arrival and you will quickly settle in. You have a great excuse for dinner out – the kitchen is a bit small – and you can barbecue, too. The Gatehouse has walls partly exposed, with spiral stairs and a very pretty roof with beams in a wheel-and-spokes pattern. Some of the furniture is antique, some not; walls are attractively plain, doors are wooden and studded. The trees all around, and the Virginia creeper, are mighty. Unusual and undeniably interesting.

sleeps	2 + 2 children.
price	£270–£300.
rooms	Each turret: 1 double with shower & wc. Living room downstairs with sofabed for smaller children. Also folding bed.
closed	Never.

booking details

	Yvonne Sargent
tel	01782 393239
fax	01782 394590
e-mail	yasargent@hotmail.com
web	www.caverswallcastle.co.uk

 map 6   entry 76

Coach House Studio
Walberswick, Suffolk

The sweeping watercolour sky of Suffolk's coast gathers Walberswick in its vast embrace. Just beyond the gate are the sand dunes and sea and the River Blyth – so gentle that the ferry is just a rowing boat. It is clapboard huts and houses peppered among the dunes and along the river, and along the other bank, a chaotic line of huts and workshops, honest and fragile; Walberswick is sleepy and beguiling, a haven for artists. The Studio is a haven, too: simple, peaceful, comfortable and bright. The mood is pine and 'country cottage', all in good solid taste. You arrive via a wooden staircase that ascends an old coach house, pinkwashed below and clapboarded above. There's a little lobby, then the light and airy sitting room/kitchen with every modern device (including CD player and CDs). The bedroom has a pine double bed – colourful and attractive. There are views across the marshes to the river and harbour, a small courtyard with garden furniture (teak with dark green parasol), and towels for tea, body and beach. The main house is opposite, with a large garden and mature trees – all so close to the sea and the superb pub that you need go nowhere else.

sleeps	2.
price	£200-£300.
rooms	1 double with bath & wc.
closed	Never.

booking details

Cathryn & John Simpson

tel	01502 723384
fax	01502 723384
e-mail	ferryhouse.walberswick@virgin.net
web	www.ferryhouse-walberswick.com

Grove Cottages
Edwardstone, Suffolk

It's impossible to do justice to the five 'nests' that make up Grove Cottages, so here's a taster. Open fires, hand-made kitchens and bathrooms, sisal floors, bright kilim rugs, pink velvet chair by the range, organic home-made honey, jams and soaps, little, dotty and adorable dogs, a welcome pack with Lavenham bakery bread, proper coffee, butter, eggs and local newspaper...The rustically romantic 300-year-old outbuildings that huddle around Grove Farm are described by Mark and Stefanie as "Suffolk meets New York loft": his sense of theatre – he's a film director – and her Scandinavian flair are an inspired mix. And the comfort is sublime. Choose a love nest of your own or take over the whole place with friends – you can eat communally and can ask Mark to barbecue a side of lamb for you all to share (in the courtyard gardens scented with herbs, quite a treat). You'll find all the essentials in the 'walk-thru' (firewood, kindling and charcoal, deckchairs, washing machine, driers), and Mark has put together an invaluable 'insider's guide' to the pubs, walks, towns and villages. Take one of the bikes that are freely available or hire a canoe to explore the countryside that artist John Constable made famous.

sleeps	4-5; 2-4; 2-3; 2; 2.
price	£150-£727.
rooms	**Orchard** 2 doubles, 1 with extra single; bath & wc. **Gun** 1 double; 1 bunk-bed; bath & wc. **Bakery** 1 double with extra single; bath & wc. **Rose** & **Snow** both 1 double; bath & wc.
closed	Never.

booking details

Mark Scott & Stefanie Wege

tel	01787 211115
fax	01787 211511
e-mail	stefanie@edwardstone.demon.co.uk
web	www.grove-cottages.co.uk

map 4   entry 78

The Barn

Farm Lane, Sussex

Walk along the golden sands of Camber. Then retreat to The Barn for an immersion in the taste and imagination of the Holts. They have worked a rare magic on this building, filling it with light, colour, space and a sense of fun. Driftwood has been taken from the beach and used to great effect for shelving, quirky old furniture has been mixed with new, and the wooden deck for *al fresco* meals is an attraction in itself. The very modern kitchen is a corner of the vast open living room; above it is a gallery with a double bed, curtained for privacy. The main floor is stripped wood with a hessian rug and there's a woodburning stove for winter cosiness. Black and white photos on the walls, sheets and towels of Egyptian cotton, plain white china and a basket of food waiting for you should you order one. Georgina is a rushed-off-her-feet mother, wonderfully friendly and helpful with two small and delightful children; yours may on occasion share her child-friendly garden, though you also have your own big lawn. Georgina will even cook you a delicious dinner and bring it to your door.

sleeps	6.
price	£525–£800.
rooms	3: 1 double with bath & wc; 1 double; 1 twin; bath & wc.
closed	Never.

booking details

	Georgina & Richard Holt
tel	01797 225202
e-mail	gholt@atlas.co.uk
web	www.camberbarn.co.uk

Garden Cottage
Blackwell, Warwickshire

Hard to believe that this idyllic Cotswold cottage was once a hay loft above and stable below. It's still upside-down with bedrooms below, kitchen and sitting room above – an arrangement Liz has made the most of to suit disabled guests, who have a stair lift and a specially equipped bathroom. Off the stone-flagged hall through latched wooden doors are two large, beamy, double bedrooms, warm and inviting with pastel walls, chintz and patchwork quilts. Wardrobes are huge. The old potting shed makes a generous third double with a good, big bathroom – it's a conversion that really works. Upstairs to fabulous timbered walls and ceilings, comfy sofas and doors to the balcony overlooking strutting bantams, and fields beyond. Lots of good eating places nearby – though your fresh white-walled kitchen is a joy to use. Footpaths and bridleways radiate in every direction, and gardeners are wonderfully near such treasures as Hidcote, Kiftsgate, Upton House and Coughton Court. The honey-stone villages of Chipping Campden and Broadway are close, too. *Distillers Cottage, for 2 (wheelchair friendly) also available.*

sleeps	4-6.
price	£300-£550.
rooms	3: 1 double with bath, shower & wc; 1 double with shower & wc; 1 twin with bath, shower & wc.
closed	Never.

booking details

	Liz Vernon Miller
tel	01608 682357
fax	01608 682856
e-mail	sawdays@blackwellgrange.co.uk
web	www.blackwellgrange.co.uk

map 3   entry 80

The Dower House
Winsley, Wiltshire

An American guest comes regularly and sends her luggage and provisions in advance: the Dower House is her "English country seat". Which says it all – this is the lap of well-mannered luxury (though if six of you stay here then it is also great value). Elizabeth and John Denning have set themselves the highest standards and manage to meet them; they are superbly hospitable and run things with style and panache. The feel is traditional 'country-house', so the sitting room has chintz on the sofas and chairs, floor-length curtains with pelmet in similar style, plain carpet and mahogany furniture. There is an elegant dining room supported by a modern and impeccably equipped kitchen. The bedrooms are lavish and similarly comfortable: coronets with drapes over the beds, deep pile carpet. To the front of the house are the manor lawns; to the back is the walled patio and garden, private and delightful and a safe place to keep small children. In spite of all the luxury the house does have a lived-in feel. A short walk through the old village takes you to the pub. The splendid medieval manor, where the Dennings live, is across the lawn.

sleeps	6.
price	£700.
rooms	3 doubles with bath & wc.
closed	Never.

booking details

John & Elizabeth Denning

tel	01225 723557
fax	01225 723113
e-mail	burghope.manor@virgin.net
web	www.burghope.co.uk/Self-Catering.htm

Sleightholmedale Cottages

Kirkbymoorside, Yorkshire

The gardens are the essence of this lovely place; ask Rosanna and you can sit, read and walk in them – heaven. You live cheek-by-jowl in a line of six little cottages, once the stables and outhouses for the Lodge, sharing the criss-cross gravelled courtyard space with others. Or book them all for Granny's 80th birthday party. Rosanna is hugely helpful and happy to start you off with some shopping and fresh flowers. Each cottage is plain, practical, modest, perfectly comfortable for a holiday. There are pine banisters, fitted kitchens, a miscellany of furniture, mostly new, some IKEA cloth rugs, posters and prints, books and watercolours and cheerful cushions. The light floods in through ceiling-to-wall windows. The Archway has the best sitting room view, the Stable Cottage has its own patio; three cottages have open fires. But it is primarily for the setting, the countryside and the gardens that you come. At night the darkness is deep and you can see the stars. This is an SSSI, a beef-breeding grassland of 150 acres where you can walk without footpaths, fish for trout or watch the horses and other animals. *Shared laundry with honesty box.*

sleeps	4-6 per cottage.
price	£205-£420.
rooms	6 cottages sleeping 4-6; phone for details.
closed	December-February.

booking details

Mrs Rosanna James

tel	01751 431942
fax	01751 430106
e-mail	wshoot@aol.com

map 7   entry 82

2 Riverside

Wharfedale, Yorkshire

Perched on the river bank beside the magnificent five-arch bridge at Burnsall, this upside-down cottage is reached through the courtyard of the famous Red Lion. The accommodation is compact, the décor spanking new. Wallpapered bedrooms on the ground floor are floral or striped and have supremely comfortable beds and crisply laundered sheets; the gleaming white bathroom is decked out in a jolly, nautical vein. Upstairs, the brightly-tiled kitchen has a blue and yellow theme, and the sitting room is deliciously snug and homely. The village is renowned for being unspoilt – little has changed for centuries; as a result, visitors can outnumber inhabitants (who total 90): this is a popular spot! The fell views and the gentle sound of tumbling water will entrance you; anglers will appreciate the private fishing – grayling and trout abound; walkers are spoiled for choice. Here is some of Yorkshire's most magnificent scenery and the Dales Way on the doorstep. The mullion-windowed Red Lion just next door cossets with good food and a commendable cellar.

sleeps	4.
price	£240-£435.
rooms	2: 1 double; 1 twin; bath & wc.
closed	Never.

booking details

Elizabeth & Andrew Grayshon

tel	01756 720204
fax	01756 720292
e-mail	redlion@daelnet.co.uk
web	www.redlion.co.uk

Applebarn Cottage
Westwood Drive, Yorkshire

Enclosed cottage gardens for toddlers, big lower garden for older ones, hosts who have two little girls of their own, and goldfish, rabbits, hens... here are the makings of a perfect family holiday. Tim and Paula are deeply committed to their nearly-new holiday home venture and clearly love doing what they do best. Each cottage is 'Victorian heritage' in style; each delightfully different. Westwood, once the coachman's house, has a roomy terracotta and blue sitting/dining room (where once the horses stood!) and gas-flame fire, and a charming fresh tiled kitchen. Applebarn is where the garden produce was stored – now with two roll-top baths and all mod cons. Orchard was home to the housekeeper: a roomy but cosy sitting/dining room with wing-back sofa and open log fire, white-painted brass bed, old mirrored wardrobe, colourful cushions; French windows lead to a private garden with barbecue. Welcome packs, emergency baskets, central heating, bed linen, towels, drying room, laundry, spa, bar and gym: all is included. The place is a breath of fresh air, and Ilkley a woodland walk away – visit Betty's for the best teas in Yorkshire. *See entry 85.*

sleeps	5-6.
price	£415-£595.
rooms	1 double with shower & wc; 1 double & 2 singles with bath, shower & wc; bath, shower & wc.
closed	Never.

booking details

Tim Edwards
tel   01943 433430
fax   01934 433431
e-mail   welcome@westwoodlodge.co.uk
web   www.westwoodlodge.co.uk

map 6   entry 84

Moorview, Glenmoor & Wells apartments

Westwood Drive, Yorkshire

An unusual mix of courtyard cottages and comfortable apartments that share gym, sauna, spa and bar – it works brilliantly. Tim and Paula escaped the "corporate treadmill" to fulfill a dream – what were once College of Housecraft rooms in this neo-Gothic mansion have become sumptuous Grade II-listed flats perfect for couples. Up the stairs, past the stained-glass window (magnificent), to three softly plush apartments on the second floor. Glenmoor is the biggest (sleeps four in two bedrooms), with open plan living, dining and kitchen rooms, bedrooms painted warm colours, superb moor views. Moorview has cream walls, sofas that cascade with cushions, a smart Shaker-style kitchen, more views. Wells is exquisite: heavy tartan drapes, candlesticks on gleaming sideboard, muslin-hung beechwood four-poster. The welcome pack includes wine and crusty bread; the emergency basket toothbrush and tights (two shades). Through the cattle-grid to Ilkley Moor for a blast of fresh air; back to crackling logs and good cheer in the main house with piano and honesty bar. Ilkley – genteel long before Harrogate ever was – is a 'nipper bus' or walk away. *See entry 84.*

sleeps	**Moorview** 2.
	Glenmoor 4.
	Wells 2.
price	£365–£455.
rooms	**Moorview** 1 double; shower & wc.
	Glenmoor 2 doubles with bath & wc.
	Wells 1 four-poster with bath & wc.
closed	Never.

booking details

	Tim Edwards
tel	01943 433430
fax	01943 433431
e-mail	welcome@westwoodlodge.co.uk
web	www.westwoodlodge.co.uk

Oats Royd Barn

Luddenden, Yorkshire

Banality and bad taste have been banished with this model transformation – it is fresh, light, airy, modern, stimulating and ingenious. A loft apartment in the sense normally applied to city centre warehouse developments, this one is in the former wagon house of a Victorian woollen mill in the glorious Luddenden Dean Valley. There are some extraordinary touches: Japanese-style screens round the raised double bed, metal and perspex stairs leading to a cosy twin roof room, a tall industrial flue rising from a Scandinavian woodburner – high-tech meeting old timbers. Marvellous chunky beams, wide-planked floors, original art on subtle walls (except in the bathroom, a blaze of yellow and turquoise), good books, fresh flowers. Hilly and Dan are both designers and it shows in their fascinating home too, where they do B&B (tasty meals can be arranged). You have gorgeous views of mill pond and wildlife – a decked area with seating is planned – and can set off on spectacular walks from the door. Hebden Bridge or Halifax are 10 minutes away for good eating and entertainment, buses stop right outside, and you can be collected from the railway station – just ask.

sleeps	4-5 + baby.
price	£280-£380.
rooms	2: 1 double; 1 twin; bath & wc; sofabed downstairs.
closed	Never.

booking details

	Hilly & Dan Fletcher
tel	01422 881436
fax	01422 885724
e-mail	hilly@oatsroydbarn.co.uk
web	www.oatsroydbarn.co.uk

map 6   entry 86

Photography by Michael Busse[l]

WALES

"I must have been suffereing from some mental aberration to have believed like any old ninny that it was necessary, interesting and useful to travel abroad."

J K HUYSMAN, A REBOURS

Croes Efa

Rhydwyn, Anglesey

This tumbledown dwelling was bought in the 1930s (for £40!) and superbly converted to form this little cottage 'twixt mountains and sea. The larger room was opened to the rafters and makes a big, open, airy sitting room, cosy with an open fire. Fine cottagey fabrics, elegant furniture, china and pictures make this a stylish, single-storey retreat best suited to empty-nesters; small children are not the ideal guests! There's a dark oak table for formal meals, and a smaller table in the kitchen – where walls are traced with delicate murals – for breakfast. The Aga is lit in winter for longer stays and is supplemented by an electric cooker, but there's no dishwasher or washing machine. Bedrooms are charming and light with views of the countryside and little cottage garden with bench. There's so much here to see and do: wild walks, bird spotting, cycling, fishing off rocks; the unspoiled sands of Church Bay – which has a renowned fish restaurant and a pub – are a 10 minute walk down the road. If you've never been to Anglesey, then go; it is glorious and Croes Efa (Eve's Cross) is a delightful, deeply rural place to stay. *Children over 8 welcome.*

sleeps	4.
price	£300–£550.
rooms	2: 1 double; 1 twin; bath & wc.
closed	Never.

booking details

	Miss Diana Jaggar
tel	01932 348716
fax	01932 400677
web	www.croes-efa.co.uk

 map 5   entry 87

The Bailiff's House
Llandybie, Carmarthenshire

Relaxed, unfussy and super for families, walkers and lovers of the great, green Welsh outdoors. You have the run of 40 acres of grounds with a dramatic waterfall, and The Black Mountain a couple of miles up the road. The Jenkinses, mother and daughter, are restoring gardens and outbuildings, gently bringing this Huguenot estate back to life. Geese, hens and peacocks happily co-strut the cobbles and children like to join the morning delivery of the 'piggy bucket' to its pot-bellied recipients. The bailiff lived in the original farmhouse, stolidly set facing the courtyard and now simply comfortable: quarry tiles and Rayburn in the no-frills kitchen, a woodburning stove in the sitting room and up the open stairs three biggish bedrooms (two share a bathroom literally between them), candlewick bedspreads, the odd built-in pine cupboard, a miscellany of furniture and decent bathrooms brightly tiled. Katy can arrange meals for groups in the big barn-restaurant, and there's no shortage of things to visit locally: castles, gardens, coast. The pool table is popular too. *Five other cottages available on the same estate.*

sleeps	6-8.
price	£210-£450.
rooms	3: 1 double with extra single, with bath & wc; 1 double with extra single; 1 double; bath & wc.
closed	Never.

booking details

Katy & Carole Jenkins

tel	01269 850438
fax	01269 851275
e-mail	enquiries@theglynhirestate.com
web	www.theglynhirestate.com

Capel Dewi Uchaf Country House

Capel Dewi, Carmarthenshire

Once she had restored her 14th-century house, Freddie turned her talents to her 200-year-old labourer's cottage. The sitting room is hugely comfortable: a magnificent stone fireplace, pale colour washed beams, capacious terracotta sofas, bright rugs, books, antiques and conservatory that open onto a patio which catches the morning sun. Perfect for breakfast. A conservatory on the other side overlooks a walled and secluded garden. The kitchen is well-stocked and even has a mixer for baking and breadmaking – one of Freddie's enthusiasms. Bedrooms, built generously into the roof, with painted beams and soft green carpets, offer a combination of skylight and picture windows with romantic views. Lovely white linen contrasts with richly colourful throws and painted furniture. Free extras include a maid service, logs, use of Freddie's video library, membership to a local health club, and private fishing on the River Towy (book in advance – only two fishermen at a time). Pixilated by sheer peace, you run the risk of sharing Dylan Thomas's fate when he "got off the bus and forgot to get on again" in nearby Carmarthen Bay.

sleeps	6.
price	£595–£850.
rooms	3: 1 double with shower & wc, 1 double; 1 twin; bath, shower & wc.
closed	Occasionally.

booking details

	Fredena Burns
tel	01267 290799
fax	01267 290003
e-mail	uchaffarm@aol.com
web	walescottageholidays.uk.com

map 2   entry 89

Nantcol

Llanbedr, Gwynedd

A little girl wrote in the visitor's book: "I love the garden that goes up to the mountains"... you'll feel you've arrived at the last dwelling in the world when you reach this 14th-century longhouse at the end of a four-mile valley road. John's mother discovered the lofty, granite-built, wildly romantic hideaway in the 1940s – it was, in spite of the trees growing through the roof, love at first sight. The cow shed is now the big farmhouse kitchen with a table at least 250 years old. The gorgeous sitting room has a fireplace at each end, one a vast inglenook, surrounded by lovely squishy armchairs; it's full of authentic Welsh furniture – some pieces truly beautiful – which the Grants have collected and restored over the years. Fine paintings by local artists deck the whitewashed stone walls. Stairs lead up to a twin room with massive beams and one of the finest views in Wales, and to a panelled double with a traditional patchwork quilt on a lovely wooden bed. Children will adore their own stone stairs to the hay loft which makes a dreamy room for three. Warm, welcoming, cosy – an amazing place.

sleeps	7.
price	£380–£420.
rooms	3: 1 double; 1 twin; 1 triple; bath & wc; wc.
closed	Never.

booking details

	Stephanie & John Grant
tel	01544 327326
fax	01544 327880
e-mail	bollhouse@bigfoot.com

Court Farm

Llanthony, Monmouthshire

Where else can you wander round the ruins of a medieval priory with a pint of beer in your hand? Cordelia's Grade II* farmhouse deep in the Black Mountains is attached to the priory's 12th-century walls in the family's 270 sheep-studded acres. The self-catering wing with its imposing front door was the prior's private lodgings up to the Dissolution in 1536: history abounds. The hallway is handsomely flagged and the sitting room nicely beamed and dominated by a log-filled iron range – pure Beatrix Potter. A vase overflows with scented flowers, an antique pine table gladly seats eight, and the priory peers at you through deep-set windows. The kitchen is galley-style, and basic; no space for a washing machine or ironing board but Cordelia insists you pop next door and use hers. Through the kitchen is a small bathroom with old roll-top bath. The gorgeously carved bedhead in the double bedroom may once have been a pair of monastic doors; the massive stone lintel over the fireplace protects a 17th-century oak coffer. The second room is great for children with three beds, wardrobe and chest of drawers. Deep countryside, heavenly views, ancient peace.

sleeps	5 + baby.
price	£210-£335.
rooms	2: 1 double; 1 triple; bath & wc.
closed	Never.

booking details

	Cordelia Passmore
tel	01873 890359
e-mail	courtfarm@llanthony.co.uk
web	www.llanthony.co.uk

map 2   entry 91

Laburnham Cottage

Kilgetty, Pembrokeshire

A fabulous spot right on the lovely Cleddau estuary and on the end of the main house; it used to be the village shop when Cresswell Quay was used for loading coal bound for Holland. Unsurprisingly cottagey, the downstairs sitting room has a log-burning stove, little sofas, red carpet on terracotta and black tiles and a beautiful olive ash, handmade table (Philip's work). The kitchen, with its wood effect units, and bathroom, in cheery turquoise and yellow stripes, are just the job. You can see the river from both bedrooms: the cosy double with its chunky (also handmade) bed and pink and white *toile de Jouy*-style wallpaper and curtains; the twin, ideal for children, prettily floral. You can sit just outside at the front and watch the sun go down, or wander next door to the creeper-clad Cresselly Arms – a wonderful old pub "unchanged for nearly 100 years". Swim in the river or hire a sailing boat from Pembroke Dock, and make the most of the farm shop two miles away; this is a big area for organic farming. The Wights also have B&B guests and are on hand if needed, but happy to leave you to your own devices if not.

sleeps	4.
price	£200–£525.
rooms	2: 1 double; 1 twin; bath & wc.
closed	Christmas.

booking details

Philip Wight

tel	01646 651435
e-mail	phil@cresswellhouse.co.uk
web	www.cresswellhouse.co.uk

Trevaccoon
St David's, Pembrokeshire

Right next door to an elegant Georgian mansion, the cottage shares the spacious lawn, woodland garden for picnics and long views towards Strumble Head. It has its own slate forecourt from which the open plan main room catches the morning sun; natural fibre seagrass carpets and neutral rugs retain the light feel later in the day. Comfortable seating includes a long wooden framed sofabed in gingham with bright blue cushions and there's a highly efficient electric fire that masquerades as an old stove. More gingham in the bedroom with the king-size bed, and an antique wardrobe and Victorian chair in dove-grey to match the curtains; the second bedroom has two bunks and a single bed. Both have restful views, either to the Irish Sea or to rooftops and woods. All units and appliances in the spotless kitchen area are new, and there's a pretty pale blue bathroom with shower cubicle off the sitting room. The National Park coastal path and unspoilt beaches on your doorstep, croquet in the grounds, and a pottery studio that's available to anyone keen to have a go. Additional friends or family can B&B next door.

sleeps	5 + baby.
price	£200–£475.
rooms	2: 1 double; 1 room with single and bunks; shower & wc.
closed	Never.

booking details

	Caroline Flynn
tel	01348 831438
fax	01348 831438
e-mail	flynn@trevaccoon.co.uk
web	www.trevaccoon.co.uk

map 1   entry 93

Penpont

Brecon, Powys

A cat idles in the cobbled courtyard. An old sheepdog rests with its head on its paws. You could imagine you were in a French château: the roofs are slated, the walls a comforting patchwork of old stone, plants and bushes. Yet this is deep in Wales. Swing open the old door and a staircase takes you to the flat, where you are private yet remain part of this great, kindly house. The flat doesn't try to be spectacular, just cosy and human, well-decorated and generous. There's a small but comfortable sitting room with open fireplace, a place for children to laze away from the adults in the kitchen, or vice-versa. The kitchen is big — candlesticks on a sociably large table, modern kitchen units, an old dresser, bold-checked curtains — and the sight and sound of the rushing river fills the room. Bedrooms are simple, attractive, with a familial mix of old furniture, stand-alone basins and plain carpets. The river is a real draw; take a canoe if you can, spend all day teasing the waters, build a rope bridge… Behind the house is a handsome old stone bridge leading to a farm. You feel miles from anywhere.

sleeps	16.
price	£1,000–£1,200.
rooms	6: 1 quad; 1 triple; 2 doubles each with extra single; 1 twin; 1 single; 2 baths & wcs; 2 showers & wcs.
closed	Never.

booking details

Davina & Gavin Hogg

tel	01874 636202
e-mail	penpont@clara.co.uk
web	www.penpont.com

Glynmeddig

Pentrefelin, Powys

You are on the slopes of the stunning Cilieni Valley, deep in the Brecon Beacons, at the end of your own half-mile drive. Ducks cruise the pond; red kites patrol overhead. Everything here is on the generous side and our inspector loved all the space and the breathtaking views from this old converted barn. Inside, all is light and large, bare stone, old oak rafters and A-frames and some new pine. The Maughans deliberately aimed to make this conversion of an old hay barn and stables a real treat for families and a fun place for children; they also went to great lengths to preserve as many of the original materials as they could. Two huge doors made by local craftsmen lead into the bright, big sitting room into which the evening sun streams. The bedrooms under the old timbered eaves are airy and simply furnished with good storage and breathtaking views; all the doubles also have a single platform bed for children. There's underfloor heating, lashings of hot water, a boot room *and* a drying room. The young can swim in the river – it's quite safe – cycle or play tennis and football. Marvellous.

sleeps	20-24.
price	£1,500-£2,000. Weekends £640.
rooms	8: 4 doubles all with extra single; 2 twins; 2 rooms with 2 sets of bunk-beds; 3 showers; 5 wcs.
closed	Never.

booking details

	James & Punch Maughan
tel	01874 638949
fax	01874 638080
e-mail	goodmaughaning@btinternet.com
web	www.glynmeddigbarn.co.uk

map 2   entry 95

Pippins
Penybont, Powys

Nearby Cefnllys Castle used to echo to the sounds of skirmishes between the English and Welsh; nowadays a furious clucking and ruffling of chicken feathers greets you at this fine 100-year-old granary. Jackie and Peter have wisely taken full advantage of the heavenly views over the verdant Ithon Valley. It's a fun, upside-down conversion whose clean lines and warm colours are both restful and dynamic. A pine staircase leads from ground floor to large open plan sitting room – light, airy and comfortable with deliciously squishy sofas in warm rustic tones and bright rugs on polished beech laminate floors. Skylights open for a summer breeze; cushioned window seats encourage daydreaming as you gaze onto sheep-strewn hills. A beechwood-surfaced kitchen at the far end is well-equipped. Bedrooms are downstairs and done up in simple country style with Designer Guild throws on cottagey beds; bathrooms are modern and stylish. There's masses to keep you fit: walking, pony trekking, golf... even fishing on your private stretch of river.
Children over 4 welcome

sleeps	4.
price	£190–£320.
rooms	2: 1 double with shower & wc; 1 twin; shower & wc.
closed	Occasionally.

booking details

Peter & Jackie Longley

tel	01597 851032
fax	01597 851034
e-mail	jackie@neuaddfarm.fsnet.co.uk
web	www.neuaddfarm.co.uk

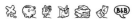

Photography by Michael Busselle

SCOTLAND

"What would the world be, once bereft
Of wet and of wildness? Let them be left,
O let them be left, wildness and wet;
Long live the weeds and the wilderness yet."
GERALD MANLEY HOPKINS, INVERSNAID

Lower West Elchies
Fraserburgh, Aberdeenshire

Fishing is the thing in the land of the River Spey and here you have a solid fishing lodge in its own 90 wooded and watery acres. Make the most of your delightful *ghillie* (fishing or hunting guide) and his wife Morag, happy to do a 'welcome shop' if you ask. You are in a fine, open position looking onto the neatest fields you have ever seen, and a shortish drive (or longish walk) to the pretty village of Aberlour. The lodge is extremely well maintained. Leaping salmon hang above the fireplace, a rack for wet togs above the Rayburn. The sitting room is traditional, with cream walls and a sofa in slate-blue velour; it has a nice, gentlemanly feel. Sensible bedrooms have mahogany chests of drawers, fresh blue and white duvet covers, terracotta-patterned curtains and blinds on new windows. Walk the Speyside Way, trek up Ben Rinnes... or fish: spey-casting (a thrilling sport, by all accounts) was born 150 years ago on the hurtling waters of the Spey. No wonder some fishing lodges are booked decades in advance – you can also fish the trout ponds for free. *Log cabin at Rinnes View also available.*

sleeps	6-8.
price	From £412.
rooms	4: 1 double; 1 twin, 2 singles; bath & wc; shower & wc.
closed	Never.

booking details

	Margaret Adams
tel	01346 510891
fax	01346 510891
e-mail	fishing@elchies.demon.co.uk

Ardtornish

Oban, Argyll

Golden eagles have been seen soaring, as have sea eagles. Over a hundred other types of bird have been spotted. Otter, pine martens, wild cats and deer – both red and roe – roam the estate. Trout from sea and loch await your line, and, of course, salmon. You will see nothing out of place, no crime, no pollution – and you will feel not a twinge of stress. It is a heavenly place, far far from everything. Yet the big house and its dependent buildings are an island of civilisation in 60 square miles of highland wilderness – pure and unspoiled. The 'special places' here are scattered among the main Victorian house and its estate houses and cottages. Some are vast and almost baronial, especially those in the big house, others more cosy and separate; some are modernised, others not. When you book, take time to find which one is right for you; the selection is astonishing and the people running the place quite delightful. (The estate management is, by the way, progressive and unusual.) At the end of the loch is the Sound of Mull – another vast playground for lovers of the outdoors.

sleeps	4-20 per unit; 90 in total.
price	£235-£1,060.
rooms	Victorian mansion house, estate houses & cottages. 12 units in total.
closed	Never.

booking details

John Montgomery

tel	01967 421288
fax	01967 421211
e-mail	tourism@ardtornish.co.uk
web	www.ardtornish.com

map 9   entry 98

The Tower at Greenwood

Ardslignish, Argyll

You may even see an otter in the loch; certainly seals and all manner of birds. It is a vast expanse of great beauty and long views to woodland and distant hills, rugged and unspoiled. The tower is unusual, built by Richard himself on the corner of their own house, specially for self-catering. So you will not be surprised to find that it is spankingly modern inside, with everything Tourist Board approved. From their own woods have come the ash for the little dining table, the Scots pine for the windy stair, the oak for the beams, and the logs – amply supplied – for the woodburner. There's a CD player, books and a superbly equipped, tiny kitchen; underfloor heating ensures warm toes. There's a deep tub in the bathroom and a very fine circular double bedroom with simple chintz curtains and big balcony for glorious views. From this remarkable place you can walk straight into the woods, onto the hillsides, into the waters of the loch. Borrow bikes or a little boat for a day (or hire it for longer), pay for rucksack lunches, have the edges taken off the ruggedness. Superb in any season; skiing is a drive away.

sleeps	2.
price	£250-£350.
rooms	1 double with bath & wc.
closed	Never.

booking details

Lois & Richard Livett

tel	01972 500201
fax	01972 500701
e-mail	loislivett@ardnamurchan.com
web	www.ardnamurchan.com/tower

Fenders
Aberlady, East Lothian

The castle is hugely grand; delightful and more informal Fenders is close by. Two 18th-century stone cottages (formerly the homes of the Head Gardener and the Head Forester) have combined to make one. Fenders, built into the medieval wall that runs through the estate, has its own, secluded garden; step through gorgeous woods to the castle's roses and fruit garden built by Napoleonic prisoners-of-war. Being two cottages turned into one Fenders retains two kitchens and has a sitting room plus cosy family room with log fire... so, masses of space. Lovely sea views too. Furnishings are traditional, with prints and pictures on the walls; facilities, including dishwasher, are excellent; three bedrooms have their own washbasins and the bathrooms are downstairs. All around are woodland walks; Nigel Tranter, famous Scottish historical writer, lived on the estate for 40 years and would wander the nearby dunes to gather inspiration. The situation is tremendous: five minutes from bird-rich Aberlady Bay and so close to pretty villages, castles and country houses. *Quarry House (sleeps 8) and Stable Apartment (sleeps 6) also available.*

sleeps	12.
price	£600–£900.
rooms	6: 1 double; 1 twin with shower & wc; 4 twins; 1 bath/shower & wc.
closed	Never.

booking details

	Anna Hope
tel	01875 870218
fax	01875 870730
e-mail	info@luffnesscastle.co.uk
web	www.luffnesscastle.co.uk

map 10   entry 100

Hope Cottage
Stenton, East Lothian

The low-slung little annexe to the 18th-century Hope Cottage was built of rich red sandstone to house one, or even, two, of the local weavers. The one-storey home is granny-cosy, but not granny-stuffy – far from it. Rooms are not palatial but most stylish, and have a delightfully warm, relaxed feel. Snuggle down in the terracotta sitting room by the log fire with a good book (there's an entire wall of them to choose from) while the children – or dogs, both are welcome – frolic in your little patch of secluded garden (with table and chairs.) The double bedroom is compact but beautiful with dark green walls, Black Watch tartan bed, *broderie anglaise*-edged pillows, soft lighting; the twin too is lovely. Family photos dotted around add to the homely ambience. Stenton is a conservation village between the Lammermuir Hills and the sea; on its tiny village green the old 'tron' for weighing fleeces still stands. Heather, ever thoughtful, has provided maps and guides for jaunts further afield and the mellow countryside is well worth exploring. There's golf, of course… and sandy beaches, glorious walks, and Edinburgh half an hour away. *Nightly rates also available.*

sleeps	4-5 + baby.
price	£350-£400.
rooms	2: 1 small double; 1 twin; 1 single z-bed; bath & wc.
closed	Never.

booking details

	Peter & Heather Allen
tel	01368 850293

59 High Street
Crail, Fife

Not for giants or those in the habit of stomping upstairs in seven-league boots. N. 59 is the teeniest of fishermen's cottages, a diminutive hideaway of fairy-tale charm, old stones and polished blue door, cosying up to its neighbours on the High Street. But there's room enough here for you and me in the snug four-poster, and baby makes three in the cot alongside… and another two in other rooms if need be. The furniture's cheerful, with a clean pine feel; walls are spotless white. The living area is open plan, with pine-and-white kitchen and small dining table and chairs at one end, mini-sofa and coal effect fire at the other. Fresh air types will love the setting: open the front door and you're on the High Street; stroll down the road and you're in the much-snapped and much-sketched harbour. Sleepy little Crail looks sweet enough to eat, and there are sandy beaches only five minutes away. If golf's your thing, courses abound – the splendid Royal & Ancient at St Andrews is no distance at all. Couples with children or couples without will simply love it.

sleeps	4 + baby.
price	£190–£350.
rooms	3: 1 double; 2 singles; bath & wc.
closed	Never.

booking details

J. F. & D. B. Miller

tel	01865 725203
fax	01865 725203
e-mail	john.miller13@ntlworld.com
web	www.golf-standrews.co.uk/crail

map 10   entry 102

Cambo House
Kingsbarns, Fife

It is a beautiful and vast estate, close to the pretty village of Crail. You have a rich choice: the apartments in the main house, the studios in the Gardener's Wing, or the Cottages. The main house is listed and you could fit 26 if you wish. It's a stately country-house experience; you can ask for dinners and breakfasts, too. The massive West Wing has a glorious four-poster of carved oak from a 1520s Dutch altar; the Attic is snug and dormer-windowed; the Gardener's Wing is over the archway and includes the tower. All have fine views, some even glimpses of the sea, open fires, and share washing machine, drier, sauna and games room. The one-storey cottages, two of a farmworker's row, are not a mile away: pine-furnished with log fires, field views and shared patio and lawn with a swing. The two-acre walled garden is magnificent and open to the public; the walks are wonderful and you can stroll down to the sea across the golf course. Such stability in these uncertain days: the Erskine family has been here since 1688 and in this house since 1881.

sleeps	8; 8; 6; 4; 2; 2; 4; 2-4.
price	£250-£840.
rooms	**W.Wing** double, 3 twins; bath & wc; shower; wc. **E.Wing** double, 3 twins; bath & wc; shower; wc. **Attic** 2 twins; double; bath & wc. **Parkview** 2 twins; bath, shower & wc. **Studios** double; shower & wc; and twin; shower & wc. **Cottages** twin, double; bath & wc; and twin; bath & wc.
closed	Never.

booking details

	Mr & Mrs Peter Erskine
tel	01333 450054
fax	01333 450987
e-mail	cambo@camboestate.com
web	www.camboestate.com

East Garden Cottage
Upper Largo, Fife

Two architects – both influenced by Scandinavians – decide to convert the outbuildings of their gorgeous 1830s home. It is a triumph, and wonderfully different. Downstairs is a bright, light sitting room with yellow stained wooden floors, modern paintings, comfy sofas and good books to read by the woodburner. Simple, plain and natural materials have been used but the splashes of colour are stunning; and an open plan kitchen with units of green stained wood has memorable views. The bedrooms are small but perfect with cathedral windows designed by Sue and, again, bold colours; the bathroom is sparkling. A shared, walled garden has a large trampoline and looks to sea and fabulous beaches; take the coastal path all the way to St Andrews or visit the sheltered bay of Elie with the prospect of returning to supper in one of the trendy local fish restaurants. A lovely, relaxed place with imaginative touches (a bust of Beethoven peeks out of one of the upstairs barn windows) and so much to do. This cottage is next to West Garden Cottage and an interconnecting door can be opened up, making the perfect house-party venue.

sleeps	4.
price	£260-£395.
rooms	2: 1 double; 1 twin; bath & wc.
closed	Never.

booking details

	Sue & Jeremy Eccles
tel	01333 360207
e-mail	jeremy.b.eccles@tesco.net

 map 10   entry 104

Milton Bank Cottage

St Callan's Manse, Sutherland

It's wildly beautiful up here, way in the north of Scotland. The Manse still has 60 acres of the land it was built on – for the church which still serves the community. Your cottage, with glorious views, is a super-snug base, spotlessly clean, Tourist Board approved. The sitting room has a rustically open-stonework wall at one end, comfortable sofa and chairs and a study area with books; the pine-dressed kitchen is generously-sized and has all you need, from dishwasher to Magi-Mix. Woodburners and curtains of gentle tartan add to the cosy feel. Bedrooms sit under the eaves, white-walled with velux windows and floral duvets. The bathroom has a roll-top bath. In the grassy garden, walled, safe for children, is a hammock from which to enjoy the views. You'll eat well at the pub in the village, and Rogart is an exceptional place for spotting wildlife. Wild goats are common, as are fulmar, hen harriers, buzzards, skylarks, osprey and you may even see otters. Robert and Caroline have had links with the region for over 50 years; with their help you can plan a richly rewarding holiday.

sleeps	4.
price	£150-£400.
rooms	2 twins; shower & wc; bath & wc.
closed	Occasionally.

booking details

Robert & Caroline Mills

tel	01408 641363
fax	01408 641313
web	www.miltonbankcottages.co.uk

Chez Shed

Close-to-the-edge, Isle of Iona

Beyond the fence sheep graze peacefully, as bucolic a view as one can get these days. From your decking you can admire the nearby farm outbuildings and oil tanks resplendent in their brash authenticity. The house itself leaves little to be desired, for there is little to offer. But it can honestly be described as of pure wooden construction all over, with a somewhat battered wooden roof in the same style. The main door dominates the façade of the house but there is a window on the south side and another on the north — a welcome symmetry to an otherwise ramshackle house. There is a collection of bricks for visitors, should they be taken with the urge to add another wing during their stay. There is also — and this is a superb example of host sensitivity and forethought — a spare energy source (i.e. battery) should supplies run out. Note the way the forest is beginning to encroach in a charming 'William Morris' manner, on the roof; nature will have its way here. The interior leaves something to be desired, yet simplicity may well make a comeback as a statement of fashion. Bring your own bed and furniture — so much nicer than having to change your habits to fit in with the furniture of another.

sleeps	1, with authentic discomfort.
price	Donations accepted – handywork, for example.
rooms	1 with window. Materials for DIY annexes provided.
closed	Rarely – the fork in the lock is easily removed.

booking details

	The Shedmaster
tel	Contact in person
fax	No distance correspondence
e-mail	shed@thepointofcollapse...
web	www.wobblywoodenwalls.con

map 0   entry 106

Glecknabae Cottage

North Bute, Isle of Bute

The rocky seashore and pebble beaches are five minutes by foot and the hills of Arran are across the water. The views are wonderful. The cottage – more a small house – has all this and mod cons too, and if you are wet after a long day on the shore you can dry your clothes in the drying room, then warm up by the open fire. There is plenty of space but if you prefer you can have, say, grandparents in the main house B&B, so everyone will be happy. The mood is simple and friendly. It has been dictated, in part, by the needs of families and outdoor people, but there are some good pieces of furniture and a smart little kitchen. What you really come for are the views and the garden – both are superb. The island cries out to be explored by bike and you could spend days being inspired by the views. Giant boulders are strewn on the mossy floor of the woodland, whose twisted and stunted trees reflect the acid soils and the force of the prevailing winds; hazel, birch, oak and willow are a canopy for birds and deer. Yet Glasgow is so close. Iain and Margaret are friendly, full of advice, and Bute is a mellow, gentle delight.

sleeps	4 + 1 child (on folding bed in living room or 3 in twin) + baby.
price	£375-£400.
rooms	1 double; 1 twin; bath; shower; wc.
closed	Never.

booking details

Mr & Mrs Iain Gimblett

tel	01700 505655
fax	01700 505655
e-mail	glecknabae@amserve.net

Lyndale Gate Lodge
Edinbane, Isle of Skye

The sky envelops you; sea, lochs and views of distant isles surround you. The 'inkpot-style' gate lodge to the estate snuggles into a heavily wooded dip in the landscape. Inside, all is immensely comfortable – the Rayburn will be on when you arrive – and gently stylish. The living room is open plan, shared with the dining area; there's a woodburning stove (logs provided) and all mod cons, including dishwasher. A fresh, pretty, uncluttered little double bedroom is downstairs and a twin upstairs, with beds set end to end; the bathroom is blue-panelled, white-walled, sparkling. The place is made for four, but two wouldn't rattle. Views are not great here, because of the woods, but sunsets can be. There is a glorious avenue of trees down to the beach, and you can walk to the shore along a grassy track, drop your line into the sea and await results. The walking and climbing are, of course, exceptional, and you can explore Skye on a pony. With luck, you'll catch a *ceilidh* in Edinbane.

sleeps	4 + baby.
price	£275–£550.
rooms	2: 1 double; 1 twin; bath & wc.
closed	Never.

booking details

	Marcus & Linda Ridsdill–Smith
tel	01470 582329
e-mail	linda@lyndale.free-online.co.uk

map 13   entry 108

The Tower of Hallbar

Braidwood, Lanarkshire

The fortified tower house soars, via a steep dog-legged staircase within the walls, uneven and challenging. The rooms are piled above each other in a riot of Vivat Trust restoration and 16th-century stone, crowned by a parapet walkway. So, not for the infirm, infant, vertigoed, timid or tall. But for the bold, the curious and for history buffs, this is a massive treat. On the barrel-vaulted ground floor is a loo, and the small kitchen/diner, with new wood, Belfast sink and marble tops, and good china. Up the stairs to the Hall, white with dark and handsome furniture, a log-burning stove, doorways to duck and a beamed ceiling charmingly painted with heraldic motifs. Then a single room with a deep wall recess and white bathroom. The twin and double are on the top two floors, with thick, exposed stone walls, solid antiques, soft lighting, thick hangings. The setting is wooded, between two burns and a home for badger and deer; there's outdoor furniture, table tennis and hammocks. Braidwood is not special but Glasgow is, and close enough for you to enjoy. *Small cottage with wheelchair access also available.*

sleeps	7 + 1 baby.
price	£575–£845
rooms	5: 1 double; 1 twin; 3 singles; bath & wc; shower & wc; wc.
closed	Never.

booking details

	Vivat Trust
tel	0845 090 0194
fax	0845 090 0174
e-mail	enquiries@vivat.org.uk
web	www.vivat.org.uk

20a Dean Terrace
Edinburgh, Midlothian

Across the Stockbridge would stroll the sheep and cattle en route to market. The waters of the Leith flow by in front of the house. It is fashionable, desirable, delectable – a brilliant conversion of the servants' basement in this Georgian townhouse. Your sitting room gazes upon a small patio with flowers, where you can set up a barbecue if you wish. Your double bed is a four-poster, your sofabed queen-size, your pillowcase hand-embroidered and your toiletries Crabtree & Evelyn. Colefax & Fowler have been here too. There's a bright yellow passage, antique furniture, plenty of books and a small kitchen with everything you could possibly need, including white china and a fleet of wine glasses. You can stroll along the river to St Bernard's Well and, in the other direction, to the Port of Leith. You are 10 minutes' walking from the centre of the city and close to the Botanic Gardens. Fiona and Colin are easy-going and immensely kind. Altogether a marvellously practical yet sumptuous launch pad for life in the vibrant capital.

sleeps	4-6.
price	£150-£170 per night.
rooms	2: 1 double with bath & wc; 1 twin with shower & wc; wc; sofabed in drawing room.
closed	Never.

booking details

Mrs Fiona Mitchell-Rose

tel	0131 332 2755
fax	0131 343 3648
e-mail	seven.danubestreet@virgin.net
web	www.aboutedinburgh.com/deanterrace

map 10   entry 110

The Gled

Doune, Perth & Kinross

Roses climb the 17th-century walls; your own garden, then a field and you are at the tower which marks the exact east-west centre point of Scotland – Edinburgh and Glasgow airports are less than an hour away. You are on the edge of the Loch Lomond Natural Park; not a sound to be heard except the morning curlews and the evening carousing of roe deer. The views are south from your sun porch and across the fields to the distant Gargunnock Hills. The bedrooms – big, chintzy and with antique furniture – are at opposite ends of the cottage, so family disputes are bearable! (Marital disputes, too, for the double is super-king-size and can be converted into twins in dire extremis...) It is all so comfortable and thoughtful: towels are provided and if the duvets are not enough there are electric blankets. In winter you can snuggle up to the open fire in the big sitting room. Dinner can be ordered in the cottage from menus and include shortbreads, fruit cakes, marmalades, soups, pâtés, main courses; you can even stroll over to the main house, Mackeanston, for a superb dinner.

sleeps	4-5 + baby.
price	£350-£450.
rooms	2: 1 double with bath & wc; 1 twin; bath & wc; camp bed also available.
closed	Never.

booking details

	Fiona & Colin Graham
tel	01786 850213
fax	01786 850414
e-mail	cottage@mackeanstonhouse.co.uk
web	www.mackeanstonhouse.co.uk

Rose Cottage

Dunalastair Estate, Perth & Kinross

Rose Cottage — well-named, its front is rose-draped in June — stands in a secluded garden crammed with colourful shrubs. It is part of the huge Dunalastair Highland Estate owned by the de Sales la Terrière family for over 100 years; in its heyday, the estate had its own post office and school. You don't have to stray far for romantic views of lochs lined with birch trees and the famous Schiehallion Mountain. Your little holiday home is cheerfully decorated and practical, perfect for dogs and wet wellies and fishing gear; super for young children too. There's a Rayburn in the kitchen and a lino floor, a jolly floral PVC tablecloth, fresh walls and vegetable-motif tiles; you arrive to shortbread, milk and garden flowers. The sitting room is carpeted and rugged, with good plain furniture, fireplace and basket of logs; bedrooms are neat and spotless. No family heirlooms here, just tranquillity, privacy, and a sweet garden. Borrow a boat and fish (the store in Pitlochry hires out the gear), roam the estate, play tennis. Pony trekking, white water rafting and golf are a phone call away. *Seven more cottages available.*

sleeps	5.
price	£257–£499.
rooms	3: 1 double; 1 twin; 1 single; bath & wc.
closed	Never.

booking details

	Mrs Melanie MacIntyre
tel	01882 632314
fax	01882 632491
e-mail	dunalastair@sol.co.uk
web	www.dunalastair.com

map 9   entry 112

Gardener's Cottage

Kirkmichael, Perth & Kinross

A splendid wedding present, given to Douglas's grandmother in 1912. It has glorious views all around – of the Perthshire Hills and the mountains of Ben y Glo towards Pitlochry – fantastic walks from the door and a dreamy, sheltered, child-safe garden leading down (via a five-barred gate) to a blissful burn – perfect for paddling. The house has a thoroughly friendly feel: sunny south-facing rooms with floral curtains, an easy mix of old and modern furniture in the bedrooms, a good, long bath in the freshly decorated bathroom, no shortage of wood and coal to burn in the cosy sitting room – just the spot for poring over the maps and books. Games are laid on, too, and there's no TV to rankle. And off the dining room, with its extra sitting space, is the bright, extremely functional, kitchen. The village shop/café/post office is definitely worth a mention as it provides everything from cakes to cash, vegetables, meat (you can pre-order fresh local supplies) and mountain bikes. So, come for peace and plenty of space, both in and out. There's tennis too; if you'd like to play, just ask.

sleeps	5.
price	£330–£480.
rooms	2: 1 double; 1 triple; bath & wc.
closed	Never.

booking details

Sarah Nicholson

tel	0131 552 8595
fax	0131 551 6675
e-mail	inverleithbandb@yahoo.com

Old Dairy
Alyth, Perth & Kinross

Like many fine old Scottish buildings this one is brighter inside than out: there's a pleasing mix of old (flagstones, shelving, slate slabs) and new (some IKEA). The old dairy is comfortable rather than luxurious. The twin has simple creamy walls, modern brass beds, white internal shutters and colourful curtains. In the double room, terracotta walls and white curtains at fine sash windows that bring in every splash of light. The living room is modern pine-panelled with plain walls above and a woodburner; the kitchen has a Belfast sink under the window, white walls, handsome old green-painted shelving and floors of old slab with attractive rugs. It is perfect for children: no stairs and they can play on the lawns. You can roam freely; the estate around includes an SSSI (beavers are being reintroduced) and Paul is a keen conservationist who enjoys discussing his plans. This is a great walking area, thick with hedgerows and wildlife, and Blairgowrie has all you need. It is a particularly lovely place — and mild — out of season. And you can always nip into Edinburgh if desperate for a brush with cosmopolitan life.

sleeps	5.
price	£185-£425.
rooms	3: 1 double; 1 twin; 1 single; bath & wc.
closed	Never.

booking details

Paul & Louise Ramsay

tel	01828 632992
fax	01828 632992
e-mail	louiseramsay@bamff.demon.co.uk
web	www.bamff.co.uk

map 10   entry 114

Marlee House
Kinloch, Perth & Kinross

Your "mildly grand" quarters are in the 18th-century west wing of an old and lovely 1484 manor house – ideal for two child-free couples, say the delightfully un-grand owners. This is Scottish country-house living at its elegant best: paintwork gleams, fabrics glow and there's not a frayed carpet edge in sight. The large, traditional kitchen/dining room contains all you are likely to need, from dishwasher to canteen of silver-plate; there's even a fish kettle should you have a lucky day on the river. Deep luxury in the sitting room: yellow walls, soft lights, generous cream drapes; cosiness in the double: little white-shuttered windows, sofa, *toile de Jouy*-adorned bed, bookcase, mahogany desk. The twin is more 'country' with white walls and wicker chairs and chintz floral curtains; the single on the ground floor has an exquisite muslin-draped bedhead. White bathrooms are carpeted and have mountains of towels. And the grounds: 190 acres of farmland and lochs, woods and waterfalls in which to fish, hill-walk or dream. Golfers will be happy and there are some excellent bistros in Blairgowrie. Bring the barbour.

sleeps	5.
price	£900–£1,150.
rooms	3: 1 double with bath & wc; 1 twin with bath & wc; 1 single with shower & wc.
closed	Christmas & New Year.

booking details

	Kenneth & Nicolette Lumsden
tel	01250 884216

The Old Smiddy
Stanley, Perth & Kinross

Vida is an avid traveller and it shows: her 230-year-old Scottish cottage is alive with mementos from trips abroad – and books, maps, jigsaws, crystals and big bunches of home-dried flowers. An atmospheric jumble of tables and chairs, teddies on the sofa and a whiff of essential oils (she is an aromatherapist). This is Vida's home, and if you want to take over the whole place, she will move into one of the connecting studios. Keen cooks will love the kitchen, with an Aga and an old pine dresser and herbs, spices and provisions: use what you want and replace before you go. The long sitting room has an oak dining table at one end and vast inglenook at the other. Nothing surprising about the bedrooms – white walls, coloured towels on beds, the odd patchwork quilt or appliqué bedcover. A strip of garden separates cottage from country road (you are surrounded by fields) and at the back is a large lawn bordered by shrubs and dotted with hens – the source of your organic breakfast eggs. Excellent wooden tables and chairs outside; make the most of them for candlelit *al fresco* meals. *Bookings outside peak season charged on B&B basis.*

sleeps	6.
price	£495-£625.
rooms	3: 2 doubles both with shower & wc; 1 twin with bath & wc.
closed	Never.

booking details

Vida Chapman
tel	01250 883236
fax	01250 883236
e-mail	holidays@oldsmiddy.com
web	www.oldsmiddy.com

map 10   entry 116

The Cloister House

Melrose, Roxburghshire

A treat for the ecclesiastically minded, with the abbey ruins and churchyard in view, but also for all those who enjoy beautiful places. It's a smallish sandstone building and remarkably roomy inside. All the furniture is of high quality and it feels rather like a small Georgian country house, particularly the dining room with its boarded floor, beautiful sideboard and handsome table and chairs. The kitchen is white, and immaculate. Bedrooms have richly decorated wallpaper or plain colours; one bathroom is cork-floored and striped, with a bright white rattan chair, another is bare-boarded, roll-top-bathed, terracotta-walled, with views across the graveyard to woods beyond. In winter you can idle by the coal fire in the plush brocade-and-velvet drawing room and write your novel at the desk while the children play pool in the games room. Outside, on the little gravelled yard, good outdoor furniture in front of the railings that stand between house and graveyard. Melrose is a pretty little town and there is masses to buy and do there. Run by the inimitable Vivat Trust, this is their largest property.

sleeps	8 + 1 baby.
price	£645–£1,015.
rooms	4: 2 doubles; 2 twins; 2 bath & wc; 2 wcs.
closed	Never.

booking details

	Vivat Trust
tel	0845 090 0194
fax	0845 090 0174
e–mail	enquiries@vivat.org.uk
web	www.vivat.org.uk

WHAT'S IN THE BACK OF THE BOOK? ...

FARMERS' MARKETS

Think Local
Buy Local
Eat Local

National Association of
FARMERS MARKETS

In the five years since the first UK Farmers' Market was started in Bath, September 1997, numbers have grown to over 450. Farmers' Markets are different from other markets in that they offer locally grown produce direct from the producer to the customer, thereby ensuring freshness, quality, taste and traceability.

On high days and holidays, markets may put on special events such as cookery demonstrations, hog roasts and entertainers and musicians to enhance the already congenial atmosphere. Many markets will provide recipe cards to ensure that you get the best from the seasonal produce and the stall-holders will willingly offer ideas on how to prepare less familiar items.

Make the most of British food by buying local asparagus in late spring, then tasty summer soft fruits – some turned into mouth-watering icecreams, yogurts or preserves for later in the year. In autumn look forward to trying some of over 60 native varieties of apples, celebrated with Apple Day in October. You will find all that you need for Christmas dinner at the December markets; Farmers' Markets also encourage the continuation and development of local specialities that are produced in quantities too small to be of interest to supermarkets.

FARMERS' MARKETS

anic Rainbow Trout

At Farmers' Markets local producers are selling their own products directly to customers and so are able discuss what has happened to the food before it is bought. Shoppers are directly supporting the farmers by ensuring that they get a fair price for their goods, in some instances proving a lifeline for businesses that were struggling to survive. The farmers also welcome the feedback from their customers and have been known to try new ideas as a result of this dialogue.

It is interesting to watch customers at the market rediscovering the pleasure of sociable shopping – having a chat with friends as they queue for their fish, sharing a joke with the producers as they weigh out their vegetables. It is satisfying to go home happy in the knowledge that you have procured bags full of fresh wholesome produce.

Do your bit to help to maintain our green and pleasant land by shopping at a Farmers' Market near you. It's fun!

For details of where to find Farmers' Markets please visit our web site: www.farmersmarkets.net/visit or send a large stamped addressed envelope to:

NAFM
South Vaults
Green Park Station
Bath
BA1 1JB

BIKING

Below is a selection of addresses and telephone numbers of bike hire shops around the country, which you may find useful:

England

Cornwall
Elm Farm Cycle Hire, Elm Farm, Nancekuke, Redruth, TR16 5UF
Tel: 01209 891498

Cumbria
Country Lanes Cycle Centre, The Railway Station, Windermere, Cumbria LA23 1AH
Tel: 01539 444544

Devon
Saddles & Paddles Cycle Store, 4 Kings Wharf, The Quay, Exeter, EX2 4PA
Tel: 01392 424241

Gloucestershire
Country Lanes Cycle Centre, The Railway Station, Moreton-in-Marsh, GL56 0AA
Tel: 01608 650065

Hampshire
Country Lanes Cycle Centre, The Railway Carriage, Brockenhurst Station, Brockenhurst, SO42 7TW
Tel: 01590 622627

Shropshire
Stuart Barkley Cycles, Salop Road, Oswestry, Shropshire SY11 2NU
Tel: 01691 658705

Wales

Gwynedd
RH Roberts Cycles, 7/9 High Street, Bala, LL23 7AG
Tel: 01678 520252

Powys
Cycles Irfon, Unit 2, Maesydre, Benlah Road, Llanwrtyd Wells, Powys LD5 4BA
Tel: 01591 610710

Scotland

Highlands
Off Beat Bikes, 117 High Street, Fort William, PH33 6DG
Tel: 01397 704008

www.sustrans.org.uk
www.ctc.org.uk
www.yha.org.uk

Get there by bike!

NATIONAL
cycle
NETWORK

The National Cycle Network is 10,000 miles of routes throughout the UK due to be completed by 2005. Linking towns and cities with the countryside on quiet roads and traffic-free paths, the Network offers a great way to explore Britain.

Longer-distance sections, ideal for a weekend break or holidays, are covered by an award-winning range of maps.

Alternatively, view the on-line mapping at **www.sustrans.org.uk** or call Sustrans, the charity behind the Network on **0117 929 0888**

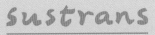

Sustrans

routes for people

PUBS & INNS

Fancy eating out or just grabbing a quick pint?
These are all hand-picked inns from our book,
British Hotels, Inns & Other Places.

England

Berkshire Crown & Garter, Great Common, Inkpen, Hungerford
01488 668325

Cornwall Halzephron, Gunwalloe, Helston 01326 240406

Trengilly Wartha Inn, Nancenoy, Constantine, Falmouth
01326 340332

The Port Gaverne Hotel, Port Gaverne, Nr. Port Isaac
01208 880244

The Mill House Inn, Trebarwith, Nr. Tintagel
01840 770200

Cumbria The Pheasant, Bassenthwaite Lake, Nr. Cockermouth
017687 76234

The King George IV Inn, Eskdale, Holmrook
01946 723262

Old Dungeon Ghyll, Great Langdale, Ambleside
015394 37272

Devon The Arundell Arms, Lifton
01566 784666

The Hoops Country Inn & Hotel, Horns Cross, Bideford
01237 451222

The Rising Sun Hotel, Harbourside, Lynmouth
01598 753223

The Masons Arms Inn, Knowstone, South Molton
01398 341231

Kings Arms, Stockland, Nr. Honiton
01404 881361

Dorset The Fox Inn, Corscombe, Nr. Dorchester
01935 891330

The Acorn Inn, Evershot, Dorchester
01935 83228

PUBS & INNS

The Museum Inn, Farnham, Nr. Blandford Forum
01725 516261

Durham — Rose and Crown, Romaldkirk, Barnard Castle
01833 650213

Essex — The Bell Inn & Hill House, High Rd, Horndon-on-the-Hill
01375 642463

Gloucestershire — The New Inn At Coln, Coln St-Aldwyns, Nr. Cirencester
01285 750651

The White Hart Inn & Restaurant, High Street, Winchcombe
01242 602359

The Fox Inn, Lower Oddington, Nr. Moreton-in-Marsh
01451 870555

The Churchill Inn, Paxford, Chipping Campden
01386 594000

Kent — The Ringlestone Inn, Ringlestone Hamlet, Nr. Harrietsham
01622 859900

Lancashire — The Inn at Whitewell, Whitewell, Clitheroe
01200 448222

London — The Victoria, 10 West Temple Sheen
0208 876 4238

Norfolk — The Lifeboat Inn, Ship Lane, Thornham
01485 512236

Saracens Head, Wolterton, Erpingham
01263 768909

Northamptonshire — The Falcon Hotel, Castle Ashby, Nr. Northampton
01604 696200

Northumberland — The Tankerville Arms Hotel, Cottage Road, Wooler
01668 281581

The Pheasant Inn, Stannersburn, Kielder Water
01434 240382

Oxfordshire — Falkland Arms, Great Tew, Chipping Norton
01608 683653

The Lamb Inn, Sheep Street, Burford
01993 823155

PUBS & INNS

The Old Trout Hotel, 29-30 Lower High Street, Thame
01844 212146

Stonor Hotel, Stonor
01491 638866

Somerset

The Crown Hotel, Exford
01643 831554

The Royal Oak Inn, Withypool, Exmoor National Park
01643 831506/7

Greyhound Inn, Staple Fitzpaine, Taunton
01823 480227

The George, Norton St. Philip, Bath
01373 834224

Suffolk

The Dolphin, Peace Place, Thorpeness, Aldeburgh
01728 454994

Sussex

The Griffin Inn, Fletching, Nr. Uckfield
01825 722890

Warwickshire

The Howard Arms, Lower Green, Ilmington
01608 682226

The Fox and Goose, Armscote, Nr. Stratford-upon-Avon
01608 682293

Wiltshire

The Red Lion, High Street, Lacock
01249 730456

The Angel Inn, Hindon
01747 820696

The Compasses Inn, Lower Chicksgrove, Tisbury
01722 714318

Yorkshire

The Boar's Head Hotel, Ripley Castle Estate, Harrogate
01423 771888

The Red Lion, By the Bridge at Burnsall, Nr. Skipton
01756 720204

The Blue Lion, East Witton, Nr. Leyburn
1969 624273

The Abbey Inn, Byland Abbey, Coxwold
01347 868204

PUBS & INNS

The Star Inn, Harome, Nr. Helmsley
01439 770397

The White Swan, Market Place, Pickering
01751 472288

Wales

Denbighshire West Arms Hotel, Llanarmon Dyffryn Ceiriog
01691 600665

Monmouthshire The Bell at Skenfrith, Skenfrith
01600 750235

Powys The Felin Fach Griffin, Felin Fach, Brecon
01874 620111

Ty Siarad, Pontdolgoch, Nr. Cearsws
01686 688919

Scotland

Fife The Inn at Lathones, Lathones, St Andrews
01334 840494

Wester Ross Applecross Inn, Shore Street, Applecross
01520 744262

Highland Glenelg Inn, Glenelg, By Kyle of Lochalsh
01599 522273

Isle of Skye Stein Inn, Stein, Waternish
01470 592362

Perth & Kinross Loch Tummel Inn, Strathtummel, Pitlochry
01882 634272

WHAT IS ALASTAIR SAWDAY PUBLISHING?

A dozen or more of us work in two converted barns on a farm near Bristol, close enough to the city for a bicycle ride and far enough for a silence broken only by horses and the occasional passage of a tractor. Some editors work in the countries they write about, e.g. France; others work from the UK but are based outside the office. We enjoy each other's company, celebrate every event possible and work in an easy-going but committed environment.

These books owe their style and mood to Alastair's miscellaneous career and his interest in the community and the environment. He has taught overseas, worked with refugees, run development projects abroad, founded a travel company and several environmental organisations. There has been a slightly mad streak evident throughout, not least in his driving of a waste-paper-collection lorry for a year, the manning of stalls at jumble sales and the pursuit of causes long before they were considered sane.

These books owe their style and mood to Alastair's miscellaneous career and his interest in the community and the environment

Back to the travel company: trying to take his clients to eat and sleep in places that were not owned by corporations and assorted bandits he found dozens of very special places in France – farms, châteaux, etc – a list that grew into the first book, French Bed and Breakfast. It was a celebration of 'real' places to stay and the remarkable people who run them.

The publishing company grew from that first and rather whimsical French book. It started as a mild crusade, and there it stays – full of 'attitude', and the more appealing for it. For we still celebrate the unusual, the beautiful, the individual. We are passionate about rejecting the banal, the ugly, the pompous and the indifferent and we are passionate too about 'real' food. Alastair is a trustee of the Soil Association and keen to promote organic growing and consuming by owners and visitors.

It is a source of deep pleasure to us to know that there are many thousands of people who share our views. We are by no means alone in trumpeting the virtues of resisting the destruction and uniformity of so much of our culture – and the cultures of other nations, too.

We run a company in which people and values matter. We love to hear of new friendships between those in the book and those using it, and to know that there are many people – among them farmers – who have been enabled to pursue their decent lives thanks to the extra income the book brings them.

WWW.SPECIALPLACESTOSTAY.COM

Britain

France

Ireland

Italy

Portugal

Spain...

all in one place!

On the unfathomable and often unnavigable sea of internet accommodation pages, those who have discovered **www.specialplacestostay.com** have found it to be an island of reliability. Not only will you find a database full of honest, trustworthy, up-to-date information about Special Places to Stay across Europe, but also:

- Links to the web sites of well over a thousand places from the series
- Colourful, clickable, interactive maps to help you find the right place
- The facility to make most bookings by e-mail – even if you don't have e-mail yourself
- Online purchasing of our books, securely and cheaply
- Regular, exclusive special offers on titles from the series
- The latest news about future editions, new titles and new places
- The chance to participate in the evolution of the site and the books

The site is constantly evolving and is frequently updated. We've revised our maps, adding more useful and interesting links, providing news, updates and special features that won't appear anywhere else but in our window on the worldwide web.

Just as with our printed guides, your feedback counts, so when you've surfed all this and you still want more, let us know – this site has been planted with room to grow.

Russell Wilkinson, Web Producer
website@specialplacestostay.com

If you'd like to receive news and updates about our books by e-mail, send a message to newsletter@specialplacestostay.com

ALASTAIR SAWDAY'S

French Bed & Breakfast
Edition 8
£15.99

British Bed & Breakfast
Edition 7
£14.99

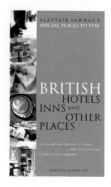

**British Hotels, Inns
& Other Places**
Edition 4
£12.99

**French Hotels, Inns
& Other Places**
Edition 2
£11.99

French Holiday Homes
Edition 1
£11.99

Paris Hotels
Edition 3
£8.95

www.specialpla

SPECIAL PLACES TO STAY SERIES

**Bed & Breakfast for
Garden Lovers**
Edition 2
£14.99

London
Edition 1
£9.99

Ireland
Edition 3
£10.95

Spain
Edition 4
£11.95

Italy
Edition 2
£11.95

Portugal
Edition 3
£8.95

cestostay.com

THE LITTLE EARTH BOOK

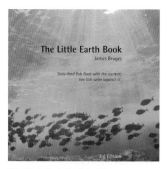

The Little Earth Book
James Bruges

'Only dead fish float with the current;
live fish swim against it'.

3rd Edition

"The Little Earth Book is different.
And instructive. And even fun!"
Jonathon Porritt

A fascinating read. The earth is now desperately vulnerable; so are we. Original, stimulating short essays about what is going wrong with our planet, and about the greatest challenge of our century: how to save the Earth for us all. It is succinct, yet intellectually credible, well-referenced, wry yet deadly serious.

Our earth is little enough to be very vulnerable. And so are we. What's happening to it? What can we do?

Researched and written by a Bristol architect, James Bruges, The Little Earth Book is a clarion call to action, a stimulating collection of short essays on today's most important environmental concerns, from global warming and poisoned food to unfettered economic growth, Third World debt, genes and 'superbugs'. Undogmatic but sure-footed, the style is light, explaining complex issues with easy language, illustrations and cartoons. Ideas are developed chapter by chapter, yet each one stands alone. It is an easy browse.

The Little Earth Book provides hope, with new ideas and examples of people swimming against the current, for bold ideas that work in practice. It is a book as important as it is original. Learn about the issues and join the most important debate of this century.

Did you know…
* If everyone adopted the Western lifestyle we would need five earths to support us?
* In 50 years the US has — with intensive pesticide use — doubled the amount of crops lost to pests?
* Environmental disasters have already created more than 80 MILLION refugees?

www.littleearth.co.uk

THE LITTLE FOOD BOOK

Our own livelihoods are at risk – from the food we eat. Original, stimulating, mini-essays about what is wrong with our food today, and about the greatest challenge of the new century: how to produce enough food without further damaging our health, the environment and vulnerable countries. Written by Craig Sams, Chairman of the Soil Association, it is concise, deeply informative and an important contribution to the great food debate. Just like The Little Earth Book, this is pithy, yet intellectually credible, wry yet deadly serious.

The Little Food Book
An explosive account of the food we eat today

Craig Sams

There is room for optimism – but you need to read this engrossing little book first!

* Brilliant and easy-to-read synthesis of complex subjects
* Pertinent – food is a daily issue – organics, GM crops, farming practices, healthy eating
* Especially timely – the decline of the rural economy, foot and mouth, changes to the CAP
* Compact size – an excellent Christmas present or stocking filler

Extracts from book:
* "In the UK alone 25,000,000 kilos of pesticides are sprayed on food every year."
* "In 2001 the World Trade Organisation fined the EU $120 million for suggesting that US meat imports should label the presence of hormones residues."
* "Aspartame is a neurotoxin that probably causes as much brain damage as mobile phone use."
* "300,000 Americans a year die of obesity."
* "Research indicates that MSG is a contributing factor in Alzheimer's disease."
* "Globally, the market for organic food in 2001 exceeded $20 billion."

www.littleearth.co.uk/food

REPORT FORM

Book title: _____

Entry no: _____ Edition no: _____

New recommendation: _____

Country: _____

Name of property: _____

Address: _____
_____
_____

Postcode: _____

Tel: _____

Date of stay: _____

Comments: _____
_____
_____

From: _____

Address: _____
_____
_____

Postcode: _____

Tel: _____

Email: _____

Please send the completed form to:

Alastair Sawday Publishing,
The Home Farm Stables, Barrow Gurney, Bristol BS48 3RW
or go to www.specialplacestostay.com and click on 'contact'.

Thank you.

BHH1

ORDER FORM UK

All these books are available in major bookshops or you may order them direct. Post and packaging are FREE.

		Price	No. copies
French Bed & Breakfast	Edition 8	£15.99	
French Hotels, Inns and other places	Edition 2	£11.99	
French Holiday Homes	Edition 1	£11.99	
Paris Hotels	Edition 3	£8.95	
British Bed & Breakfast	Edition 7	£14.99	
British Hotels, Inns and other places	Edition 4	£12.99	
British Holiday Homes	Edition 1	£9.99	
Bed & Breakfast for Garden Lovers	Edition 2	£14.99	
London	Edition 1	£9.99	
Ireland	Edition 3	£10.95	
Spain	Edition 4	£11.95	
Portugal	Edition 3	£8.95	
Italy	Edition 2	£11.95	
The Little Earth Book	Edition 3	£6.99	
The Little Food Book	Edition 1	£6.99	
Please make cheques payable to Alastair Sawday Publishing	Total £		

Please send cheques to: Alastair Sawday Publishing,
The Home Farm Stables, Barrow Gurney, Bristol BS48 3RW.
For credit card orders call 01275 464891 or order directly
from our website **www.specialplacestostay.com**

Title _____ First name _____

Surname _____

Address _____

_____

_____

Postcode _____

Tel _____

If you do not wish to receive mail from other
like-minded companies, please tick here ☐

If you would prefer not to receive information about
special offers on our books, please tick here ☐

BHH1

ORDER FORM USA

All these books are available at your local bookstore, or you may order direct. Allow two to three weeks for delivery.

		Price	No. copies
Portugal	Edition 1	$14.95	
Spain	Edition 4	$19.95	
Ireland	Edition 3	$17.95	
Paris Hotels	Edition 3	$14.95	
French Hotels, Inns and other places	Edition 2	$19.95	
French Bed & Breakfast	Edition 8	$19.95	
French Holiday Homes	Edition 1	$17.95	
British Hotels, Inns and other places	Edition 4	$17.95	
British Bed & Breakfast	Edition 7	$19.95	
London	Edition 1	$12.95	
Italy	Edition 2	$17.95	
	Total $		

Shipping in the continental USA: $3.95 for one book,
$4.95 for two books, $5.95 for three or more books.
Outside continental USA, call (800) 243-0495 for prices.
For delivery to AK, CA, CO, CT, FL, GA, IL, IN, KS, MI, MN, MO, NE,
NM, NC, OK, SC, TN, TX, VA, and WA, please add appropriate sales tax.

Please make checks payable to:
The Globe Pequot Press   **Total $** [   ]

To order by phone with MasterCard or Visa: (800) 243-0495,
9am to 5pm EST; by fax: (800) 820-2329, 24 hours;
through our web site: **www.globe-pequot.com**; or by mail:
The Globe Pequot Press, P.O. Box 480, Guilford, CT 06437

Date

Name

Address

Town

State

Zip code

Tel

Fax

BHH1

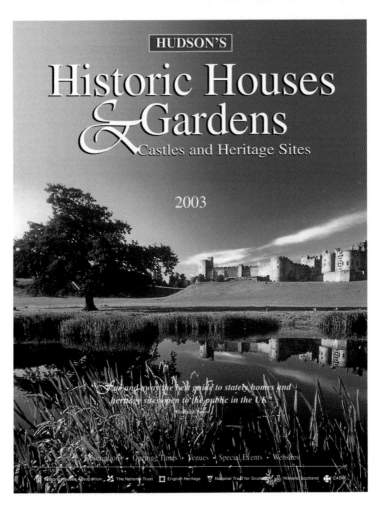

Discover the best-selling, definitive annual heritage guide to Britain's castles, stately homes and gardens open to the public.

600 pages featuring 2000 properties with
more than 1500 colour photographs.
An invaluable reference source <u>and</u> a good read.

QUICK REFERENCE INDICES

Wheelchair friendly

If you need houses which are wheelchair-friendly, contact these owners.

England
Cornwall • 3 • Devon • 27 • 35 • Gloucestershire • 44 • 45 • Northumberland • 59 • Shropshire • 66 • Somerset • 72 • Suffolk • 78 • Warwickshire • 80 •

Wales
Anglesey • 87 • Carmarthenshire • 88 • Pembrokeshire • 93 • Powys • 95 •

Scotland
Lanarkshire • 109 •

Limited mobility

England
Cornwall • 5 • 7 • Derbyshire • 17 • Devon • 24 • 30 • 33 • 35 • Essex • 40 • Gloucestershire • 42 • 44 • Lincolnshire • 49 • Norfolk • 52 • Northumberland • 53 • Oxfordshire • 62 • Sussex • 79 •

Wales
Anglesey • 87 •

Scotland
Highland • 105 • Lanarkshire • 109 • Perth & Kinross • 111 • 115 •

Properties for 2–4

England
Cornwall • 3 • 5 • 7 • 9 • Cumbria • 11 • 12 • 13 • Derbyshire • 14 • 15 • 16 • 17 • 18 • 20 • Devon • 23 • 24 • 25 • 26 • 27 • 28 • 29 • 31 • Dorset • 37 • 38 • Durham • 39 • Essex • 41 • Gloucestershire • 42 • 43 • 44 • 45 • Herefordshire • 47 • Kent • 48 • Lincolnshire • 64 • 65 • 67 • 68 • Somerset • 69 • 70 • 73 • 74 • Staffordshire • 76 • Suffolk • 77 • 78 • Warwickshire • 80 • Yorkshire • 82 • 83 • 85 • 86 •

Wales
Anglesey • 87 • Pembrokeshire • 92 • Powys • 96 •

Scotland
Argyll • 98 • 99 • East Lothian • 101 • Fife • 102 • 104 • Highland • 105 • Isle of Bute • 107 • Isle of Skye • 108 • Midlothian • 110 • 111 •

QUICK REFERENCE INDICES

QUICK REFERENCE INDICES

Wales
Carmarthenshire • 88 • Powys • 94 • 95 •

Scotland
Aberdeenshire • 97 • Argyll & Bute • 98 • East Lothian • 100 •
Fife • 103 • Scottish Borders • 117 •

Pets welcome Your pets are welcome at these places.

England
Berkshire • 1 • Cornwall • 2 • 4 • 6 • 7 • Cumbria • 12 • 13 •
Derbyshire • 14 • 15 • 17 • 19 • Devon • 22 • 24 • 25 • 27 •
29 • 30 • 33 • 34 • Essex • 40 • Gloucestershire • 42 • 43 •
Hampshire • 46 • Herefordshire • 47 • Kent • 48 • Lincolnshire • 49 •
Norfolk • 50 • Northumberland • 54 • 59 • Oxfordshire • 61 •
Shropshire • 65 • 67 • Somerset • 69 • 72 • 73 • Staffordshire • 76 •
Suffolk • 78 • Sussex • 79 • Yorkshire • 82 • 83 • 84 •

Wales
Anglesey • 87 • Gwynedd • 90 • Pembrokeshire • 93 • Powys • 95 •

Scotland
Argyll & Bute • 98 • East Lothian • 101 • Fife • 103 • 104 •
Highland • 105 • Lanarkshire • 109 • Perth & Kinross • 111 •
112 • 114 • 115 • 116 • Scottish Borders • 117 •

Welcome box These houses provide a welcome box for you.

England
Cornwall • 7 • 8 • 9 • Cumbria • 11 • 12 • 13 •
Derbyshire • 16 • 20 • Devon • 23 • 24 • 25 • 27 • 28 • 30 •
31 • 32 • 33 • Dorset • 36 • Durham • 39 • Essex • 40 • 41 •
Gloucestershire • 42 • 43 • 44 • Hampshire • 46 • Kent • 48 •
Lincolnshire • 49 • Northumberland • 58 • Oxfordshire • 62 •
Shropshire • 63 • 64 • 65 • 68 • Somerset • 69 • 70 • 71 •
Suffolk • 78 • Warwickshire • 80 • Yorkshire • 83 • 84 • 85 •

Wales
Carmarthenshire • 89 •

Scotland
Aberdeenshire • 97 • Argyll & Bute • 99 • East Lothian • 101 •
Fife • 102 • 104 • Lanarkshire • 109 • Perth & Kinross • 112 •
Scottish Borders • 117 •

QUICK REFERENCE INDICES

Pubs & restaurants

These owners have told us that there are pubs or restaurants nearby.

England

Berkshire • 1 • Cornwall • 2 • 3 • 4 • 5 • 6 • 8 • 9 •
Cumbria • 11 • 12 • 13 • Derbyshire • 18 • 19 • 20 •
Devon • 22 • 24 • 25 • 26 • 27 • 28 • 33 • Dorset • 37 • 38 •
Durham • 39 • Essex • 40 • Gloucestershire • 43 • 45 •
Kent • 48 • Lincolnshire • 49 • Norfolk • 50 • 52 •
Northumberland • 54 • 56 • 58 • 59 • Oxfordshire • 61 • 62 •
Shropshire • 64 • 66 • Somerset • 69 • 70 • 71 •
Staffordshire • 76 • Suffolk • 77 • 78 • Warwickshire • 80 •
Wiltshire • 81 • Yorkshire • 82 • 83 • 84 • Yorkshire • 85 • 86 •

Wales

Anglesey • 87 • Carmarthenshire • 89 • Gwynedd • 90 •
Monmouthshire • 91 • Pembrokeshire • 92 • 93 •
Powys • 94 • 95 • 96 •

Scotland

East Lothian • 100 • 101 • Fife • 102 • 103 •
Highland • 105 • Isle of Skye • 108 • Midlothian • 110 •
Perth & Kinross • 111 • 112 • 113 • 114 • 115 • 116 •
Scottish Borders • 117 •

Tennis

There's a tennis court in the grounds of these houses.

England

Cornwall • 2 • 4 • 7 • Devon • 22 • 31 • 32 • Norfolk • 51 • 52 •
Northumberland • 58 • Sussex • 79 • Yorkshire • 82 •

Wales

Powys • 94 • 95 •

Scotland

Fife • 103 • Perthshire • 112 • 113 •

Pool

These are houses with a swimming pool in the grounds.

England

Cornwall • 5 • 7 • Devon • 25 • Essex • 40 • Gloucestershire • 45 •
Northumberland • 58 • Somerset • 74 • 75 •

Wales

Carmarthenshire • 89 •

PLACE NAME INDEX

EXCHANGE RATE TABLE

£ Sterling	US $	Euro €
1	1.57	1.60
5	7.83	8.0
7	10.96	11.2
10	15.66	16
15	23.48	24
17	26.61	27.2
20	31.31	32
25	39.14	40
30	46.97	48
35	54.79	56
40	62.62	64
45	70.45	72
50	78.28	80
70	109.58	112
90	140.90	144

Prices correct at going to press October 2002.

EXPLANATION OF SYMBOLS

Treat each one as a guide rather than a statement of fact and check important points when booking.

Children are positively welcomed, with no age restrictions, but cots, high chairs etc are not necessarily available.

Full and approved wheelchair facilities for at least one bedroom and bathroom and access to all ground-floor common areas.

Ground-floor bedrooms for people of limited mobility.

No smoking anywhere in the house.

Pets are welcome. Check when booking.

Payment by cash or cheques only.

Working farm.

You can borrow or hire bikes.

Swimming pool on the premises.

Tennis.

Food shop nearby.

Sheets provided without extra supplement.

Weekend breaks available.

B&B also available.